"If in the early 1800s you wanted to go from Pittsburgh to the Pacific Ocean, you would have wanted Lewis and Clark as guides. If you want to plant a church—or you coach people who do—you'll want to follow the sage and mega-experienced guidance from Griffith and Easum. I've planted churches and coached hundreds of planters and I can tell you Jim and Bill know what they are talking about. The chapters on money and leadership development are alone worth the price of the book. The *Ten Most Common Mistakes Made by New Church Starts* will lead you intelligently around the most dangerous bends in the river called church planting."

TODD HUNTER, president, Alpha USA

"Griffith and Easum tell it like it is: if the only plan you've got in your back pocket reads, 'reach the lost,' you're the one who's lost. *Ten Most Common Mistakes Made by New Church Starts* is the *essential trail-guide* to starting a church. I only wish they'd written it sooner. Brilliant!"

SALLY MORGENTHALER, Shapevine.com, contributor to *Emergent Manifesto of Hope*

"When it comes to church planting, Griffith & Easum 'get it.' Every year, Jim Griffith is featured as a faculty member in our church planting major as he inspires church planters to think biblically and act missionally like no one else. Their personal experience and knowledge provide comfort and courage to our church planters to make it through the tough days because they have been there."

DOUG FAGERSTROM, president, Grand Rapids Theological Seminary

"Griffith and Easum have provided pivotal insights in the planting of Epicenter Church in Washington, D.C. Anyone considering planting a new church—both pastors and judicatory leaders—needs to read this book first. It is one of a very few *must-reads* in the field."

PAUL NIXON, author of *I Refuse to Lead a Dying Church* and pastor, EpicenterDC

"Jim Griffith and Bill Easum have put together their combined wisdom in church planting and congregation development to produce this extremely helpful book for everyone interested or involved in new church starts. By guiding us through the land mines of mistakes, they have offered a clear and comprehensive view of the work before planters."

KEVIN E. MARTIN, dean, Cathedral Church of St. Matthew

"Jim is not afraid to tell the truth about how the best intentions of good church people can go awry when it comes to new church starts. His advice is practical, positive, and real. And although it is directed at new church development, those who are trying to grow an established church will also find it to be of tremendous help. More than just a treasure trove of practical help, the book also offers a perspective on the missional position of the church today that can support and encourage those hoping, praying, and working hard for the church's renewal and growth."

JOANNE THOMSON, associate conference minister, Wisconsin Conference, United Church of Christ

"If you are not making mistakes in church planting, you are not taking any risks. Without risks you will not successfully plant. Griffith and Easum have one intent, pure and simple: to help new starts avoid hitting every pothole in the road. Reading *Ten Most Common Mistakes* will save you a lot of bruises."

BILL MALICK, National Church Multiplication Director, Christian & Missionary Alliance

"*Ten Most Common Mistakes Made by New Church Starts* is a down-to-earth guide that challenges not only church planters but also church members to focus on those who are not in church yet. It is this focus that makes churches grow healthily and expands the message of the Gospel. This book outlines clear principles that transcend issues of culture, race, and class, and that can be applied in different situations. Biblically grounded and filled with practical suggestions, realistic benchmarks, and even samples of letters and case studies, this book can be the close companion of any church planter and his/her supervisor."

NORA COLMENARES MARTINEZ, Office of Church Development, North Georgia Conference of the United Methodist Church

"I laughed and cried as I read each of the ten mistakes: laughed because I made most of them (often worse than described in the book) and cried because of the pain each caused me and those around me. The sections I found most insightful were the helps given to supervisors and coaches of planters. I seriously pray that every church planting supervisor, coach, and planter will read this and saves millions of dollars and thousands of ruined lives."

GREG WIENS, Florida state pastor, Florida Church of God Ministries, Inc.

Ten Most
COMMON
MISTAKES
Made by
NEW
CHURCH STARTS

Jim Griffith / Bill Easum

CHALICE
P R E S S
ST. LOUIS, MISSOURI

Scripture quotations, unless otherwise marked are taken from the HOLY BIBLE, NEW INTERNATIONAL VERSION®. NIV®. Copyright © 1973, 1978, 1984 by International Bible Society. Used by permission of Zondervan Publishing House. All rights reserved.

Scripture marked NASB is taken from the NEW AMERICAN STANDARD BIBLE ®, © Copyright The Lockman Foundation 1960, 1962, 1963, 1968, 1971, 1972, 1973, 1975, 1977, 1995. Used by permission.

Quotations marked Message are from *The Message* by Eugene H. Peterson, copyright (c) 1993, 1994, 1995, 1996, 2000, 2001, 2002. Used by permission of NavPress Publishing Group. All rights reserved.

Cover image: FotoSearch
Cover and interior design: Elizabeth Wright

Visit Chalice Press on the World Wide Web at
www.chalicepress.com

10 9 8 7 6 5 4 3 2   09   10   11   12   13

Library of Congress Cataloging-in-Publication Data

Griffith, Jim.
    10 most common mistakes made by new church starts / by Jim Griffith and Bill Easum.
        p. cm.
    ISBN 978-0-8272-3647-9
    1. Church development, New. I. Easum, William M., 1939- II. Title. III. Title: Ten most common mistakes made by new church starts.
    BV652.24.G75 2008
    254'.1—dc22

                                                    2007046281

Printed in United States of America

Contents

INTRODUCTION

Our Story

"Our wisdom comes from our experience, and our experience comes from our foolishness."
PLAYWRIGHT AND ACTOR SACHA GUITRY

During the first twenty-two years of my ministry, my wife (Jan) and I planted five churches. They were all "parachute drops," in which, basically, it's as if you are told, "God bless you," and thrown out of a plane, on your own with no support. Twenty-two years and five church plants later, we knelt in the living room of our home and decided we didn't want to do that anymore.

That night we prayed a desperate prayer. We asked God to redeem the pain we had experienced in those five church plants—from the sins I committed, to the mistakes I made, to the experiences we had, and to the "cul-de-sacs" of effort we got lost in—in such a way that would serve new start pastors and new start congregations and organizations around the country and bring glory to God.

It's a great and humbling experience to participate in an answer to prayer. So much so, that for the last thirteen years my ministry has been to assess, train, and coach new starts and new start pastors around the country. I've assessed more than 1,500 clergy new start candidates from dozens of agencies, trained people in more than 8,000 English-speaking projects, and coached hundreds of church plants, including working with African American, Hispanic/Latino, and Asian new start pastors. It's been a great ride so far.

But I've also conducted more than 100 autopsies on failed new starts (I stopped counting when it reached 100), and I want to tell you, there's no more gut-wrenching conversation than with a fellow servant who tells you how God called him or her to plant and yet the vision unraveled right before his or her very eyes. So my purpose in this book is to spare you some of this pain and to help you give glory to God in your church plant.

Why Should You Pay Attention to What We're Writing?

Planting five churches should make me a fairly good coach of church planters. However, I am a great coach. And I am a great coach because I (Jim) have made more mistakes than any planter on the face of the planet. I've shot all my toes off, blasted off my ankles, shattered both kneecaps, and finally said, "That's enough!"

Additionally the autopsies I've done on failed church plants have given me insights into why I made so many mistakes in the five churches I planted and what I could have done to avoid them.

My (Bill's) story is a bit different from Jim's and comes from two major learning experiences. I was a restart pastor and made the same mistakes Jim made and probably more. I also have consulted on-site with more than 600 churches over the past fifteen years, many of which were either church plants or restart churches. And those consultations taught me that Jim and I are not alone in our mistakes. Most pastors are making the same mistakes we made.

So we want to alert you to the top ten mistakes church planters make and how to avoid them.

Who Should Read This Book

Those of you who supervise church planters will find this book to be a pastoral call to you, quite honestly. You need to pastor those planters in your particular group.

Those of you who are in the discernment process of thinking about church planting, my comments are designed to sober you up.

Those of you who are already church planting will recognize yourself as we go along. If the pain gets too bad, take an aspirin or two.

How You Should Use This Book

Each section contains an explanation of one of the top ten mistakes we've seen planters make over the years. Each also contains what we've learned will fix, or undo, the mistake. We will also include coaching and supervisory sidebars. Along the way you will see a few footnotes now and then. Most of these are added for the purpose of explaining terms that might not be understood by people new to church planting and to offer information about possible resources.

This book contains the combined lessons learned by Jim Griffith, from planting five successful churches and from years of coaching church planters, as well as the wisdom Bill Easum has gleaned from almost twenty years of consulting with congregations. When possible, we will refer to one another as "we," and note the difference when necessary.

All right? Let's dive in.

1

Neglecting the Great Commandment in Pursuit of the Great Commission

"Yet I hold this against you: You have forsaken your first love."

REVELATION 2:4

Donald Grey Barnhouse, the great Presbyterian preacher, talks about the time he was visiting out of town and a pastor friend invited him to tag along to a wedding reception. Of course, Barnhouse knew no one, but he enjoyed watching the people dance and celebrate the festive occasion. As the party progressed, he noticed an elegantly dressed woman sitting all alone, unnoticed by the partygoers. Barnhouse inquired of his friend, "Who is that woman?" His friend replied, "Why, she's the bride."

This story illustrates the number one mistake planters make—in their zeal to pursue the Great Commission, they ignore the One for whom they're planting the church—God.

We've seldom met a planter who started out to put church planting before God. Most planters quickly identify God's call as the reason for their planting a church. The problem is church planting can become so all-consuming. It seduces planters into thinking that by putting it before all else they are doing God's will, but nothing should come before our love for God. The Great Commandment is first and foremost in the heart of any person who says they are a follower of God and a disciple of Jesus Christ. Replacing the Greatest with the Great, makes "God work" an obsession of the most damaging kind.

Most church planters are zealous about evangelism and committed to helping fulfill the Great Commission.[1] Nothing wrong with that. However, we've found too many pastors are doing the right thing for the wrong reason. In their pursuit of the Great Commission many have made a fatal mistake—they have neglected the Greatest Commandment.[2] A subtle, but deadly shift occurs first in the minds and then in the hearts of the planters—the thrill of church planting and reaching people and building a new faith community takes precedence over the personal responsibility to grow spiritually. Church planting becomes their obsession, blinding them to the reasons God called them in the first place.

The Great Commission minus the Great Commandment reduces evangelism to a vocation, a challenge, or a duty. However, the deep motivator for people who take evangelism seriously is an overwhelming love of God. The Great Commission is the inevitable outflow of a heart filled with a love for God. The impetus for planting a church has to be a desire for people to experience this love, not simply to carry out some mandate from the past.

---

[1] "Go into the world and make disciples" (Mt. 28:19–20, author's paraphrase).

[2] "Jesus said, 'The first in importance is, "Listen, Israel: The Lord your God is one; so love the Lord God with all your passion and prayer and intelligence and energy." And here is the second: "Love others as well as you love yourself." There is no other commandment that ranks with these'" (Mk. 12:29–31, *The Message*).

However, too many planters are seduced into trusting their own gifts and competencies. We've known many planters who could plant a good church with God no more than marginally involved. What troubles us is very few planters seem concerned about this lack of the spiritual dimension. More often their motivation is to "prove someone wrong," try a new method, dispense with some traditions, or be their own boss.

Church planting is a spiritual enterprise that can only be effectively accomplished by deeply spiritual people. Obsession with putting people in seats certainly has more appeal than setting aside time to cultivate one's love for God, but that must be done.

Rather than rely on the program *du jour,* effective and faithful planters lead from a heart overflowing with a love for God. They embody this love in all their conversations. Their goal is not to get people to come to church; their goal is to introduce people to the love of God. The goal is not to tell people how bad they are, but to tell how good God's love is.

Whenever we get with colleagues, we ask them if they've ever had a church recruit their services by saying, "We're concerned that our people don't seem to love God very much. Would you consider working with us, so that we can develop ways to increase their capacity to love?" In all our years of coaching, we've never received this kind of inquiry, nor have any of our colleagues. Instead the calls are always about how to get more people in the pew, or get troublemakers out of their church, or how to raise money.

Are you a church planter trying to love God, or a lover of God trying to plant a church?

Don't get us wrong, without people your vision will perish. But without a tender heart for God, there's no place for the vision to reside.

So, church planter, why are you so focused on planting a church? Be careful how you answer.

MISTAKE NUMBER ONE: In pursuit of the Great Commission, church planters neglect the Great(est) Commandment.

So, let us ask you a question. Are you a church planter trying to love God, or a lover of God trying to plant a church? The distinction is crucial. If you are a church planter trying to love God, God will not share glory or power with you, because God must always come first. You must be a lover of God trying to plant a church because the Great Commandment always trumps the Great Commission. We plant churches because our love for God is so strong we can't do anything else.

You can't put loving God to the side while you plant a church—no matter how much you want to change the world. If your heart for God doesn't grow, your ministry will subside and you'll find yourself spiritually shriveling up, void of any spiritual power, and that spells doom for your plant.

The Fix: Avoiding the Mistake

Planter, have you forgotten your first love, the "Bride"? If so, stop in your tracks and return to your first love. Do it now! Set aside everything and get focused once again on the Greatest Commandment.

Take a moment to focus on this word from God:

"To the angel of the church in Ephesus write: These are the words of him who holds the seven stars in his right hand and walks among the seven golden lampstands: I know your deeds, your hard work and your perseverance. I know that you cannot tolerate wicked men, that you have tested those who claim to be apostles but are not, and have found them false. You have persevered and have endured hardships for my name, and have not grown weary. Yet I hold this against you: You have forsaken your first love." (Rev. 2:1–4).

It doesn't matter how hard you work or how passionate you are about planting a church; if you forget the power behind the plant—the "Bride"—you're doomed to shrivel up and die on the vine.

One more thing about the Greatest Commandment—it tells us to love others as God has loved us. These others include your family. Don't make the mistake of so many planters and ruin your marriage over planting a church. No church is worth that.

So keep the Great Commandment first and foremost in your heart. Let that be the fountain from which springs all of your passion for everything in life, including church planting. Keeping this focus will serve you well in all that you attempt in life.

G
r
e
a
t

C
Great Commandment
m
m
i
s
s
i
o
n

■ ■ ■ SUPERVISORY COMMENTS: Don't let your planters rely on the church plant to grow their spiritual lives. It's presumptuous for the planter to think the new church will feed the planter's spiritual appetite. Many dechurched people find themselves spiritually confused, wasted, or lost, and rarely at the same spiritual level as the church planter. Also, the "details" of the new service can prove quite distracting to the new start pastor—signs posted strategically, parking attendants and greeters stationed appropriately, seating and staging arranged tastefully, not to mention the sound being right, the upfront people remembering their lines, transition points, noise from the hallways, a child crying during prayer time, ad nauseum, ad infinitum.

● ● ● COACHING COMMENTS: Planter, do two things. One, attend a vibrant, spiritually alive worship service eight to ten times a year (usually on a Sunday evening or weeknight). If you're married, take your spouse. Sit in the back row, and soak in the power of God without having to worry about anything but giving and receiving. Do not attend a church of like tribal affiliation, and do not take your children. This time is for you and your own spiritual development. Two, regularly visit with an associate or spiritual director not associated with the new start for reflection and camaraderie. Nothing is as valuable as a confidant from outside the plant.

A cousin to this mistake occurs in the form of "team meetings," which involve countless hours rehearsing the vision, values, and mission statement, not to mention all the logistical discussions. The "business" of the church trumps God every time. I've (Jim) attended launch team meetings that began on high notes of worship, prayer, teaching from the Bible, all of which are centered on the church plant, not on God. Then, after a short break, the "real" discussion starts—has someone found a nursery coordinator, how's the purchase of sound equipment going, or a review of the final three logo choices. You get the picture.

This mixing of God and details around the plant models the very pattern most planters are fleeing and everything they loathed about their former churches.

What's the solution? Separate these meetings. If you're meeting for spiritual interaction with God, then do so—and retire to the kitchen for refreshments. Meet individually with those persons responsible for various tasks in the new start. You do not need to bring people together regularly to "report" what's happening. If you do, that group will become your first church board, although unofficially.

Moving On

The persistent failure of many church planters to understand and develop the spiritual dimension, both personal and corporate, of planting a church leads us to the second biggest mistake church planters make—failure to take seriously the various forms of opposition that inevitably accompany the work of God and God's people. To that mistake we must now turn.

2

Failing to Take Opposition Seriously

> *For our struggle is not against flesh and blood, but against the rulers, against the authorities, against the powers of this dark world and against the spiritual forces of evil in the heavenly realms... Pray also for me, that whenever I open my mouth, words may be given me so that I will fearlessly make known the mystery of the gospel, for which I am an ambassador in chains. Pray that I may declare it fearlessly, as I should.*
>
> EPHESIANS 6:12, 19–20

Harry launched his plant with a really good feeling. Everything had gone more smoothly than he had dreamed. The launch was successful, the crowd was turning into a community, and all seemed right with the world. Then it happened. Without warning, and from the least likely places: some of his launch team became upset that he wasn't spending enough time with them; several neighboring pastors began complaining to Harry's supervisor that he was encroaching on their territory and stealing their people; and his supervisor began what felt like a grand inquisition into Harry's methods.

13

As if that wasn't enough, the city stopped allowing the church to place a sign in front of the school advertising their presence on Sunday. Harry's spouse came down with depression over all of the bad things that were happening to Harry. And the kids began to act out their unhappiness with the whole planting thing. What gives?

When we ask church planters to name the source of their greatest opposition, we often get this response, "I was prepared for the devil and his demons, but I was not prepared for well-meaning church people and my own tribe's bureaucrats!" Having heard this repeatedly, we began to realize several forces of opposition are recorded in the book of Acts other than the obvious one of spiritual opposition. So, let's take a look at them.

Institutional Opposition

Much of the opposition faced by planters comes from within the plant itself. Many new attendees of a church plant are church people who have relocated to the area and find themselves in need of a church "home." They look for one similar to what they left in the former place of residence. This group evaluates the church plant based on what they left and what they need, not on its missional intentions, and certainly not on its DNA. They want the "brand" they just left. And if it's not, they often don't just leave; they try to change things.

Institutional opposition also comes in the form of churches in the area that feel "threatened" by the presence of a newly forming faith community. These churches lack a Kingdom mindset and see this new church as the "competition."

I (Jim) coached a church planter who was invited to return to his hometown to start a church. The four other "evangelical" pastors in town invited him out to eat and proceeded to inquire: "Why did you come here? We don't need any more churches." This young man, a fairly strong individual, called me that night and said, "I knew the devil would greet me at the city limits, but I did not expect him to take the form of Christian colleagues."

These kind of churches are, generally speaking, relatively harmless, unless they share a denominational affinity with the new plant. If so, they can make things quite uncomfortable for the supervisor of the plant. We suggest you and your supervisor make a "courtesy call" on any affiliated churches already in the area of your new church plant, to speak to the pastor and lay leader(s) together—never just the pastor. Introduce yourself, share your heart and call, articulate your vision and style, and follow with a time for Q and A. The Bible encourages us in Romans 12:18, "if it is possible, as far as it depends on you, live at peace with everyone."

We suggest to planters that they meet the clergy in their area and explain what the project is and participate as fully as possible in appropriate ecumenical events, with the exception that the planter refrain from taking any responsibilities for such events for three years.

Cultural Opposition

Throughout the book of Acts, as the gospel migrates deeper into the known world, its messengers are met with fierce opposition from the unchurched inhabitants. This is not unlike what happens today to church planters.

Countless times, requests to rent or lease temporary facilities are sidetracked, stonewalled, or just plain turned down. Much of this is anecdotal, but multiple church planters have commented on the sense of resistance they felt from the local powers, who make it impossible to rent schools, raise church and state issues, frown on extended leases, and prevent them from buying more acreage because the church is tax exempt. While these may all be legitimate responses from the government's perspective, they certainly are frustrating to a church planter.

Spiritual Opposition

You need to understand—starting a new church is not a benign activity. Spiritual resistance is inevitable.

We're reminded of Paul's request to the Colossians: "Pray

for us, too, that God may open a door for our message, so that we may proclaim the mystery of Christ" (4:3).

Paul understood his ministry as the church's first intentional "church planter" was dependent, not on his skills or technique, but rather on the leading and empowering of the Spirit, and the prayers of the saints. Paul knew that the "battle" to bring the gospel to those who had never heard it was fought on multiple fronts, including the invisible and spiritual levels. He needed prayer and power for his message to be effective.

When one attempts to plant a church, it's not primarily about techniques. The planter is venturing into "occupied territory" only to be greeted by forces, seen and unseen, conspiring to work against any movement of God.

If you think you can march into occupied territory without resistance, you're wrong. There *will* be a clash. You can't afford to be naïve. A battle lies ahead for anyone with a vision for a biblical, loving, Christ-centered community, regardless of what kind of music or drama or special events you may or may not use.

If you want to plant a church, you will face, and must be prepared for, *spiritual warfare*.

Church planting isn't child's play, and spiritual warfare is more than just a metaphor for the conflict that occurs—emotionally, politically, philosophically. Church planting is critical, front-line, make or break it kind of stuff, and the "enemies" of the coming Kingdom want nothing more than to see good, sincere, talented, gifted, and gracious people get destroyed or wounded (or help in the destruction or wounding of others) because they're trying to do a job they simply can't do without a deep calling and sturdy prayer coverage.

Church planting is not a game, nor a challenging job, nor an opportunity to experiment with new forms of ministry. Starting a church, then leading it into maturity, is a *calling*, plain and simple. And if you aren't *called* —if you can't speak in some way to the deep, unspoken, inarticulate but clear as spring water conviction that God has spoken God's heart to yours and compelled you to this absolutely insane task—don't do it. Run, don't walk, away from it. It's just not worth it, on any level. Why?

We assure you, if you don't have that deep assurance of God's calling, presence, and *agenda,* you will crumble under the strain of them or just abandon ship and run.

We can't begin to tell you how many young would-be church-starting pastors we've seen fall to pieces under the pressure or stress or conflict.

The Fix: Avoiding the Mistake

You need intercessors to pray for you. These are individuals who possess the spiritual gift of intercession and who are outside your circle and mission and can hold you, and your family, up before God and pray for your guidance, wisdom, and the grace to lead.

Recruiting intercessors means more than just calling up people and asking them to pray for you. There's a spiritual discipline of intercession that enters a level of spiritual conflict that is inexplicably deeper and more effectual than what most of us imagine or are prepared to do.

So, here's what we propose you do.

Draft an Intercessory Prayer Team

You need to find people who are *called* to pray, believers whose primary "ministry" in their daily Christian life is to find a quiet place to offer themselves to God in prayer and intercession on your behalf. These believers are willing and able to keep praying until they have a sense that they have "prevailed."

Your intercession team needs believers who have a track record of interceding for others and seeing answers regarding protection, provision, and fruit.

They do not need to meet together or have access to e-mail or instant messaging. Just get them praying for you, and if they can do it together, so much the better.

Your team of intercessors needs to be "outside your plant" so they can pray deeply without an agenda. Being able to do so allows them some sense of objectivity as well as a sense of emotional and spiritual distance from what you and your team are doing, as well as what fires your goals, dreams, struggles, and fears.

This team should do their work in absolute secrecy and confidence. They must (and you must tell them to) take seriously Jesus' commands to pray "in a closet" and to "not let your left hand know what your right hand is doing." It's critical that you can call and ask them to pray for anything, and that nothing you ask or that they pray can ever find its way back to your plant.

Resisting the Resistance

You need to remember that a church "start up" is a migration into a "foreign climate" or "occupied territory." You will be surrounded by different values, ideas, agendas. There will be resistance, and it will come on multiple levels. And with resistance there will be enemies.

In the past, your roadblocks have probably originated with church people and the old ways they wanted to preserve. But in this new context, the resistance you experience will be more unseen than seen. It will more than likely be broad, confusing, and subtle. It will manifest itself in nearly every layer of your life, your team, and your process.

All of what we have shared with you in this chapter is about one thing: to prepare you for the resistance you will face as an emissary and missionary to an "occupied territory." Some of your new neighbors will be threatened and put off by your existence. You'll find yourself confronted on every level—culturally, spiritually, theologically, and politically. Your little experiment will bug the status quo. You will be confronted with dangers and perils you never imagined. Doors will be slammed in your face, and you may discover those closest to your heart and plan are working at cross-purposes to you.

You must resist it all! And, above all, never take any of it personally. The opposition isn't about you—it's about the Kingdom. You must never blink! Remember, "Perfect love drives out fear" (1 Jn. 4:18).Your role is to prepare for it so it doesn't take you by surprise.

■ ■ ■ SUPERVISORY COMMENTS: Supervisors set the "spiritual tone" for the behind-the-scenes prayer activities. Those supervisors who fail to understand that church planting is a struggle, a battle, will be easily misled and fail to support the church planter. Far too often, the supervisor listens to those complaining about the efforts of the church planter. There's nothing more regrettable. Your church planter needs to know that you are behind them 110 percent!

No mother worthy of the name would let an outside force attack her newborn. She would defend her baby at great peril to herself. The same is true with the supervisor. You must send a clear message to those attacking the plant that such actions will not be tolerated.

● ● ● COACHING COMMENTS: The coach must insist that one of the first actions the planter takes is to recruit an "intercessory prayer team." Have the planter tell you who each person is and set up the means necessary for the planter to communicate prayer requests on a regular basis.

Do not try to coach a project that is vulnerable to attack!

Moving On

After we pray.

3

A Love Affair with One's Fantasy Statement Blinds the Planter to the Mission Field

Sam was unhappy in his present church even though he had had some success. So many things he wanted to do were squashed by his board. He had great plans and ideas that never were implemented because of his board's unwillingness to upset the status quo. This discouraged Sam—so much so he began to think, "If I didn't have to contend with this board, I could pursue my vision." So Sam began to attend workshops sponsored by church planters and heard story after story that fed his desire to be "on his own," unencumbered by a board. He was hooked.

In time, Sam received a call to plant a church. Now, for the first time, he was sure he would be able to plant the church of his dreams. Sam resigned from his current church, attended some training events, and set out to plant a church in a new city.

Preparing for the new church plant was an absolute delight. Sam included in the vision of the new church everything he had always wanted to accomplish but hadn't been allowed to try. The new plant would have all the bells and whistles he could afford.

Nothing technological or innovative would be off limits—he would make sure of that. He would also make sure the board would be the most flexible and innovative group he could find and that his leaders would come from the ranks of those first-line innovators.

After months of planning and developing his vision, Sam chose the location of his church plant and began to gather people.

But things didn't go as Sam planned. Many of the things Sam had seen work other places didn't work in his plant. He was stumped. They were doing everything correctly. They had all the right equipment; the videos were awesome; the music was outstanding; the newly designed logo and brochures were state-of-the-art; and the leadership was open to anything he suggested. But it wasn't working. People weren't showing up, and those who did failed to return.

Sam continued undaunted by his lack of success, working harder to continually perfect the elements of his vision. Still, his grand experiment wasn't resulting in people, much less transformed people.

Two years later the plant closed, and Sam's vision died.

What happened?

Sam made a fatal mistake that many planters make. His love affair with his fantasy church blinded him to the realities of the mission field around him. His formula for success didn't match the needs of the mission field, and he was unable to adapt. Sam had created a "church in a vacuum" long before he had settled on the exact mission field. Sam was so in love with his fantasy church that he forgot to examine his real-life mission field. Consequently, he couldn't adapt his methods. He never contextualized his strategy because his methods were sacrosanct.

In reality, Sam didn't have a mission or vision statement. He had a fantasy statement, and his love affair with his vision blinded him to the realities of the mission field.

The difference between a fantasy and a vision is a fantasy never gets translated past the sheet of paper.

You see, successful planters think like missionaries. They know they are going into "occupied territory" to reach unreached people, a job for which they need to learn the language, technology, and culture of the new area. For them the mission field dictates the tactics, not the fantasy statement.

We see a lot of planters who actually compile a *fantasy statement* that bears no connection to reality whatsoever and gets passed off as a *vision statement*. The difference between the two is a fantasy statement never develops beyond the paper on which it is written.

So at the boot camps, we talk a lot of about, "It's great you've articulated your plan in writing—Hallelujah! But we want to talk to you about turning the plan into real, live people." Church planting is about going out and getting more and more people. And after that it's about gathering those people and gradually forming them into a redemptive community.

Planting a church is a process of experimentation, innovation, and replication, but always within the realities of the mission field and how it's responding. The planter has to be constantly adapting and modifying the vision to the mission field.

Planters often have such a love affair with being innovative and ideologically driven that they give little thought to the actual mission field and the key question, "What's it going to take to reach these people?" Planters and teams who make this mistake start the church based on an untested and uncontextualized fantasy, and the fantasy never materializes into enough people.

God doesn't baptize the details or the strategy, only the goal.

Effective church planters intuitively say to themselves, "This isn't working." They have a come-to-Jesus meeting internally and say to themselves, "We cannot continue down this road, we've got to adapt...NOW!"

The Mission Field Determines the Method

We don't mean to suggest that church planters don't experiment. They do, lots of times. We're referring to those planters who have such a love affair with innovation and ideology that they become gaga over it to the point that it's the center of everything they do.

Sam was hell-bent on doing video projection because his board wouldn't allow him to do it at his previous church, not to mention the fact that all megachurches use video. Sam's problem was he fixated on a method and became blind to the big picture—reaching people for Jesus Christ. Innovation plays a significant place in any effective plant, but planters can become so "inebriated" on it that they become blind to the realities of their context.

Several years ago I (Jim) was asked to conduct a "biopsy" on a struggling church plant in west Texas. Its first years were marked by healthy growth and stories similar to Acts 2. However, in year five they sent their music leaders to a "worship workshop." They had a great time and returned and began to put in place some new things they'd seen at the conference. However, the church went into turmoil and began to hemorrhage members, while also ceasing to reach any new people.

When they launched, they had used "cowboy-type" music; and the place exploded with interest. Many came because they could worship God in that genre and setting. However, now the music team introduced a different genre of music. Notice, they didn't introduce deeper ways to worship God, only different methods. Clearly, the people felt caught off guard, hoodwinked. The church went downhill fast. Of course, the more-spiritual leaders viewed this as "spiritual warfare" and began to look under all kinds of rocks.

I came in and observed that their mission field was ripe for a method that resembled what they started out with, and they should revisit the kind of music that won over so many—"country." You'd think I'd denied the existence of God, the virgin birth, and the resurrection, all in one sitting!

After a spirited discussion, they acknowledged feeling "insecure" about their style of worship, because it was so rare and everyone else was doing such "cutting edge" ministry. I pointed out to them that "fruit" is the only way to measure "cutting edge." They had overlooked the small detail that their style of music had led their church to be the third largest church in the area in just five years.

There's a fine line between "cutting edge" and "over the edge."

Over the years I've (Bill) learned to ask a question of church planters who are failing: "How many hours a week do you spend in your office?" If I get a response of more than an hour a day, I know what the problem is—they are spending valuable time tinkering with technology or perfecting their fantasy instead of spending it out among the people. It's rare for a conversion to take place in the office of a new church plant.

It takes months to develop a concept you can build a healthy church around. Often when the process is over, you're probably not where you started out, and that's okay. You haven't compromised your call; you've just made it more effective. You've contextualized your methodology to the mission field.

The apostle Paul is an excellent example of contextualizing one's approach. He arrived at the Acropolis with a message that had worked in several cities previously and was ready to unload it. As he soaked in the culture, he noticed something he hadn't encountered before—a statue to an unknown God—and he adapted his message to the context. Paul didn't change his vision or message. The message was all that was important, so if he had to adapt his style to reach the people, he was more than ready. (See Acts 17:16–34.)

God honors only those planters who love the people more than their fantasy church!

Please don't get us wrong. Nothing is wrong with innovation or technology. Use it as long as it connects with those who need to hear the good news. But if it doesn't, adapt! It's not God's will for what you're doing. It's nothing but your fantasy, and it will take you down in flames. A love affair with innovation and technology can blind the planter to the actual needs and issues of his or her mission field.

Genuine concern, care, and hard work overcome a lack of innovation and great ideas, but the opposite is not true.

We're seeing this love affair with technology and innovation a lot now because of all the workshops on media. Just remember, you may have designed some tremendous ways to communicate the glorious message of the gospel, but if you start with that and forget about a heart for your mission field, it's over.

So, here's our question: Do you love the people more than your fantasy church?

One Sure Way to Ineffectiveness and Failure: Ignore Your Mission Field's Idiosyncrasies

Because they fail to exegete the surrounding area, contextualize their approach, decide on whom to reach first, and *then* choose a methodology that will reach the targeted people, church planters often make the mistake of winding up with a church designed for "everyone." The net effect of this approach is thirty or forty people—forever!

Most mission fields have three to five very different people groups within them. Because the planter hasn't exegeted the area and determined beforehand which one of these groups to reach first, he or she winds up with a few from each group, which is seldom good because each group requires or wants something different. We often hear planters say, "We're a multicultural church," even though they only have a handful of people. Somehow they think they're effective because they have representatives from each mission field coming to their church, but that's a mistake. They now have a church for everyone, which means a church with very few distinctives.

The problem is they don't have any focus. Therefore, they don't have a consistent strategy. The strategy changes with whoever walks through the door. All of a sudden, a bunch of traditionalists come to the church and start squawking about not liking the style of music. Now what do you do? If you're a trained planter, you know the mission field always determines the type of music, but if you don't have an intentional mission field, you have no intentional strategy, and therefore, no intentional focus. And so, you listen to their complaints, you do the unthinkable, and change the style of music. And you're dead!

Several years ago I (Bill) helped plant a church that now has over five thousand in worship. The church is designed to reach non-Christian young adults who enjoy hard rock music and a casual lifestyle. The entire staff shows up in well-worn jeans and T-shirts, with some wearing flip-flops. One of the bigger givers in the early years said to the pastor, "If you don't start dressing up a bit, I'm leaving." The pastor quickly responded, "There's the door!"

So trying to put together a church that reaches everyone means your strategy is constantly changing and there's no predictability. We all know that any effective church has a predictable liturgy. Whether it's prescribed or not, it's there. And, in that liturgy, the most important factor seems to be a certain sense of predictability when it comes to the *style of music*.

The key is to analyze the mission field and decide which

group of people we should reach out to first. Usually the first group of people is those people most like you. Focus on them first, and then the next group in the area. Why make it even harder than it is? Let's at least leverage the people we might have a shot at reaching. Then, after you've reached them, leverage your resources to figure out a strategy to reach the second group in your geographical mission field.

Some people have a problem with the homogenous principle. We don't, because it's not a matter of singling out one group and ignoring another. The issue is more one of affinity rather than discrimination. Affinity is a two-way street. About 70 to 80 percent of the people who attend a church are in a fairly tight socioeconomical pattern. They choose to be at that particular church because they want to identify with the majority of the people already present. But for some reason the homogenous principle has been reduced to, "We're only going to let people in who are like us." That is not what we're saying—not at all.

Planters who begin with an ideology or methodology before exegeting the mission field greatly reduce their probability of success.

We're merely referring to leverage—trying to reach the people who are the easiest to reach and then branching out from there. If you look at most of the nonhomogenous churches in the United States, you will find that the area around them is also very diverse.

So decide who you are going to focus your attention on, and develop your strategy and your liturgy around them. Then don't blink when someone doesn't like your chosen style.

The Fix: Avoiding the Mistake

Planter, you've got to be able to take what you have on paper and turn it into people. That means two things: one, you must love the people in your area more than your fantasy church; and two, you must be willing to adapt your methods to the realities of the mission field. You must fall in love with the people, and you must exegete your mission field to the point that you understand every facet of it. You need to listen to these words on a daily basis: "When he saw the crowds, [Jesus] had compassion on them" (Mt. 9:36). It's all about people, not your fantasy church, or your expensive technology.

The same can be said for those planters who start with an ideology. One autopsy I (Jim) performed involved a group of people who shared a common belief that "home schooling" should be the preferred educational pattern for all people. They started a church around that conviction and proceeded to recruit people to their church as a means to "convert" people to their ideology. They recruited thirty or forty families and couldn't understand why they had stagnated and experienced infighting. Gradually the members drifted off, quite disillusioned with the church.

Another autopsy I (Jim) conducted was with a new start whose mission was to reach marginalized people with a gay-lesbian orientation. So they focused on being known as the "Gay" Church. It backfired for all the same reasons as the Home-School experiment. An ideologically driven new start fades because they baptize an idea or a method first, and then try to force the mission field to adjust. Nine times out of ten, the mission field gives up a handful of people to such an attempt, and the vast majority of the mission field barely notices the project.

Unfortunately, lack of interest in ideologically motivated projects often only encourages those who have bought into the idea. They interpret lack of interest as the way to justify their existence. Too often these are nothing other than a "support group" for a niche group—legitimate in their eyes and meaningful in that purpose. However, it's a mistake to call it a new church plant.

■ ■ ■ SUPERVISORY COMMENTS: Supervisor, if you have similar affinities with technology, innovation, and the latest formula and methods as your planter, you may be unable to see the project clearly and may end up promoting and defending a very bad idea.

You need to make sure the planter:

- is compelled by a burden for the people and has affinity with them;
- is compatible with the area into which he or she is going;
- thoroughly understands the area in which the church is to be planted;
- lives in the mission field.

Supervisors need to understand the area in which the church is to be planted *before* choosing the planter. Understanding the area is far more important than whether or not the denomination doesn't have a church presence in the area.

A significant number of church planters need an outside person to tell them church planting is more than a love affair with technology or a vehicle to experiment with ideas. So, don't be dazzled by the planter who comes in with some untested grand experiment. Before you fund an untested experiment or replication of some other effective church plant, make sure it fits the demographics. While every effective church plant is going to have some innovation or replication, it is imperative that you test it against the mission field. Is it working? If not, pull the plug.

Also, if the prospective church planter hasn't been able to succeed at his or her previous church, he or she probably won't be able to succeed in the new church plant. There's a difference between funding a person's experiment and funding that which they have shown the ability to do.

One of the dangers supervisors face is the growing desperation among denominational officials. Just about every denomination is in decline. The cracks are getting wider, and supervisors of church plants are becoming more desperate. Don't fund projects out of desperation.

● ● ● COACHING COMMENTS: Most often the planter will want to start with the "concepts" of the plant. As the coach, you have to force the planter to "walk the mission field." Then force the planter to come up with a definable composite of the people living there, including their lifestyles, challenges, socio-economic status, world views, voting preferences, musical preferences, etc. Forcing the planter to get specific will give you a backdrop from which to ask, "How do your methods and strategies match with this group of people?"

Constantly remind the planter to test his or her dream church with the response from the area. Help the planter see it's more important to understand and connect the methodology to the people in the area than for the planter to have all the latest technology or the idea *du jour.*

If the planter cannot move beyond his or her fixation and so fails to connect with the mission field, this will indicate it's time for you to revisit your coaching relationship with the planter.

4

Premature Launch

After a year of hard work, Jim had collected forty people in small groups and was itching to launch. He knew the maxim: "The more people you have on the first Sunday, the more likely the church will thrive." But he couldn't wait any longer. He announced that in two months they would launch.

Everything they could afford to do was done. All of the essentials were in place, and they launched. Seventy-five people showed up. Fifty-four returned the second Sunday. A year later the church was still struggling with less than fifty people.

In 1991, my (Jim's) sister-in-law gave birth prematurely at twenty-four weeks to my first nephew, Alexander. At the time he entered the world, Alex weighed one pound, fifteen ounces. The odds of surviving such an early birth are quite small, and the odds of surviving without major physical handicaps even smaller. So, you can imagine the joy in our extended family the day he came home from the hospital. To this day, he suffers a little peripheral vision limitation, but that's all. We think of him fondly as our "miracle baby."

I recall photos of Alex lying on a special platform with numerous tubes and wires attached to his tiny body. Standing behind him in the photo was a "team" of specialists solely dedicated to Alex's survival outside the womb. The specialists assigned to him 24/7 used all of their training to nurture my young nephew as he fought valiantly to develop outside the comfort of his mother's womb.

As one who has conducted dozens of autopsies on failed new starts, I'm (Jim) often asked, "What's one of the main reasons new starts fail?" Without hesitation I can say, "premature birth." The new church launches publicly with an insufficient "critical mass" of people and quickly moves from the "euphoria" of birth to the nightmare of realizing, "Sunday follows Sunday, follows Sunday, follows Sunday, follows Sunday." What started out so exhilarating and full of hope and dreams quickly shifts to "crisis" mode, focusing on survival. All the resources raised and all the people recruited now face the daunting task of resisting the downward pull of a rocket that has peaked only fifty feet off the launch pad. Again, let us repeat—one of the recurring symptoms in failed church plants is premature birth, because the new church lacks sufficient infrastructure and development to survive on such limited resources. It lacks the amount of fuel necessary to overcome the gravitational pull of inertia.

We've yet to hear a wrong reason that new churches launch too soon; they always make sense...at the time.

Every reason new churches launch too soon is a good one. Let's list them:

- The enthusiasm of the launch team—they want to make something happen. People who gravitate to church plants are high octane, much like the planter, and they're used to action and results and making an impact for God. Often their past church experiences have left them wanting more challenge, more interaction with unchurched people, more creativity, and more say in what should happen. A new church affords them that opportunity. So, along with the planter, they're anxious to be used by the Lord to build God's church.

- The planter has a "burden" to declare the mighty acts of God. Many messages from the word of God are burning inside, and the "need" to preach leaves the planter antsy to move to public meetings.
- The launch team members increase the pressure by saying their contacts remain distant about attending informal meetings, but promise to attend the new church: "Once you start meeting in a building, then we'll visit." This leaves the launch team clamoring to get started. How can the planter put off such legitimate efforts and concerns?
- Those managing the finances become concerned about the ministry expenses and outflow of monies and insist on public services to take an offering. Later, we'll devote an entire chapter to money, but for now all we'll say is starting for this reason only accelerates the outflow of money.
- The misplaced enthusiasm of the advisory committee. Most new starts have a group of excited laity and/or clergy and supervisors, who volunteer to act as "architects" and cheerleaders for the new church. They conscientiously read all the books on church planting and enthusiastically incorporate every new idea into the design, including big-hairy-audacious goals and industrious timelines. For some groups this process may go on for several years until a planter is recruited and hired. Once this happens, they even set the birth date for the "grand opening."

Listen to the story of a planter I (Jim) inherited at the two-year mark. He unpacked the moving van and moved in his family, set up a makeshift office, rented a meeting place, printed a bulletin, hired a musician, and launched for public worship...all in the same week! Many readers will have friends or colleagues who have experienced this type of new start. I (Jim) call it the "pop-up" model, where everything is in the package. All that's needed is for someone to pull the string and presto, "pop-up" church. Sadly, this model, however rightly motivated, rarely works.

- "But if we don't start proclaiming the gospel and letting people experience our redemptive community, we'll miss our 'window of opportunity.'" While we appreciate the passion and sincerity implicit in this statement, we also know that the demise of the new project will leave the mission field with "no" voice. There's a fine line between opportunity suspended and no opportunity at all.

All these reasons converge to get the launch team to say in one accord, "Let's start next week."

In our experience, many planters and their teams misunderstand the purpose of the public launch. They wrongly assume that the goal of the launch is to "get started." It's not. The goal of the launch is to get into orbit where the new church can begin to develop with minimal amounts of effort to stay aloft. This differs radically from the "grand opening" methodologies of the 1980s and '90s, where a mass-marketing campaign attracted significant numbers of people who had no prior knowledge of the new planter or project. In the new century, this method rarely produces such results. Quite to the contrary, much energy and morale and finances spent on the "grand opening" produce little or no people. Ironically, it works once the church has achieved "critical mass," but often that's several months after launch.

Planter, you are going to make lots of mistakes and survive, but launching prematurely virtually guarantees failure. This mistake is a head wound!

Every church plant needs an appropriate gestation period for a variety of reasons, but two stand out above all others: (1) to identify the contributions and limitations of the launch team members and (2) to reach a critical mass of people significant enough to populate the ministry teams and/or small groups.

You Must Have Critical Mass before Launching

It's a well-known fact that the more people collected before the church launches the more chance the church has of surviving and becoming an effective ministry. We call this collection of people a "critical mass." So what's critical mass?

Church planting is about putting people in seats; after that, it's about putting more people in more seats.

Critical mass is culture specific—that is, it's determined by the mission field itself. On one occasion, I (Jim) had a planter who was told by his supervisory committee to postpone public worship *until* he had 250 people. When I asked him to determine how many churches within a ten-mile radius of him averaged that many people in worship, he found the largest church only averaged eighty-five! Just as the baby leaving the protection of the womb too early can create severe handicaps, so staying in the womb too long creates a "toxic" reaction, leading to certain impairment.

Critical mass can also be explained by the number of cars in the parking lot that suggests something legitimate is happening inside. If you pass by a restaurant in a thriving metro area and don't see any cars in the parking lot, the restaurant isn't as appealing as one where the parking lot is full. But, if we were out in the country and passed by a diner where two cop cars and a pickup truck were in the parking lot, we might say, "This looks like a good place to eat." Critical mass is culture dependent. It is impossible to put a number to it. So, we talk about gathering enough people so that when you launch the church it appears you actually are viable with numbers.

How Churches Grow Numerically

Counting numerical growth should be kept simple in the beginning—as simple as adding one person at a time. The growth goes something like this, and it certainly isn't rocket science.

Small Church Syndrome

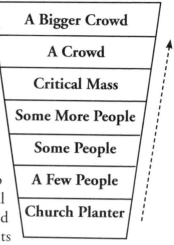

Churches that launch without critical mass seldom achieve the numbers necessary to be classified as a "crowd." Instead, they are faced with what is called the "small church syndrome." Instead of a critical mass, the church is simply an overgrown small group. The gathered group is of such insufficient numerical size that it begins subtly to defend itself by citing the benefits of its size—intimacy, connectedness, and inclusiveness. Doing so unwittingly creates a barrier, making it impossible for any new people to find their way into the young church. Then the inevitable happens—the remaining entrepreneurial leaders begin to fade away.

It's not unusual for a new start to attract and lose a high percentage of "entrepreneurs," so when one departs it's not cause for alarm. However, when they begin to leave in mass and none are joining, that signals a major problem. Failure to intervene quickly results in a "closed church."

With all of the apostolic-minded people gone, the remaining people circle the wagons and focus on their needs and expect the planter to focus on them. You know what happens next—the church hangs on for many months, if not years, justifying its existence with false thinking such as, "We really are a great group of people, and we love each other so much."

A premature launch is like a preemie baby. All the energy and money that could be used to move the church forward are now spent on just keeping up with the rent and salary, and the church never moves beyond the launch number. Every church plant will burn through large amounts of money before ever seeing a black bottom line. Launching too early actually increases the debt load, because you start with a handful of people and you're meeting weekly in a school that has a capacity for 400. It's ironic; the fewer people you begin with the more expensive the church plant becomes.

Whatever kind of church you're called to plant, you have to have a critical mass of people to add legitimacy and validity to it in the eyes of the public. If you launch with just a few people today, the church stays a handful of people tomorrow.

Calculating Your Public Launch

Like any good birth, you calculate the launch time around the three periods of development—similar to the trimesters of pregnancy. These launch development "trimesters" can be designated as preview season, exhibition season, and launch window. Let's look at each one.

Preview Season

During this season intentional events are scheduled that preview the elements of the upcoming public celebration. You don't have to have all of the elements complete or perfected in this phase of "pregnancy"—they are under development. This period of development usually lasts for six to nine months.

The preview services create

- a taste of what is to come
- worship for the team
- opportunities for the team to invite their friends
- opportunities for the involvement of already attached Christians and churches in the area
- a rehearsal opportunity to work out the programming bugs and train up front presenters

During the preview season, you follow up on the guests, develop small groups, and discover the next group of contacts to invite to the next preview service as well as motivate and enlist team members for the next preview.

We've found two liabilities to the preview events you should avoid. One, many on the launch team will want to start formal celebrations right away and not doing so may discourage some of them. Two, since each preview event requires competence and relevance, experimenting with various up front presenters could backfire.

However, the preview season is essential. Since the success of the project depends on the ability of the planter and the launch team to recruit and assimilate new people, the failure to do so during the preview stage will indicate poor planting potential.

We have found a few milestones that need to occur during the preview season:

- Multiple "taste and see" events must be hosted (more on this later).
- A "word-of-mouth" presence must be created in the mission field.
- You must add at least 25 percent new people at each preview event.
- The launch team must have gained financial ownership of the project.
- Up front presenters have been recruited and trained.
- Follow-up systems have been developed for assimilating and handing off people.
- Critical mass is achieved based on the makeup of the mission field.
- Multiple cells or small groups are developed.

Exhibition Season

In this phase the church moves to weekly celebration services that include all of the elements of the celebration at launch time, most likely on the day and the hour of what will be the regular weekly celebration.

We have found some milestones during this season that must occur before going to the actual launch celebration:

- The launch team adjusts to the new schedule.

- The assimilation process is increased and is fully developed to handle an influx of people.
- A baptism service has occurred—you have new converts.
- The critical mass has been expanded.
- The infrastructure is fully developed: people in charge of the essential ministries, team members chosen, cell groups established, follow-up strategies in place, and the necessary systems and administration help functioning. (Note: this does not include by-laws, constitutions, or chartering.)

The Public Launch

This is the time when you let the mission field know you are "open for business." We encourage you to avoid the term "Grand Opening."

Put the Launch on a Time Line

During our Boot Camps, we give the planters a "formula" by which they can set a date for going public with their churches. Sometimes this date may be as much as twelve to eighteen months away. This forces the planter to think beyond the fixation of many who want to launch "as soon as we get there."

Setting a launch date and working toward that date force the planter to determine all the steps to be accomplished *before* he or she flips the switch… Based on what we've already discussed regarding "critical mass," the planter now turns the focus to gathering people.

Wayne Cordeiro, pastor of New Hope Christian Fellowship in Honolulu, shared with me (Bill) over dinner how he decided when to plant the church. He made a list of all the people he would need in order to pull off an inspiring worship service. His list came to 180 people! Then he said, "When I had that many people trained and ready to go, I announced we would publicly launch."

The Fix: Avoiding the Mistake

What you need to do is make sure you not only have enough people and money to launch but you also have enough to thrive on into the future. Too many planters only ask, "Do we have enough money budgeted to start the church?" The problem is, once the church gets started all those unchurched people come in, but they don't give at first. Yet you still have all the overhead.

It takes longer than most planters think to turn unchurched people into spiritual givers. From the day you launch to the day you're able to sustain yourself from the gifts and offerings from your congregation usually takes months. And that's what gets planters into trouble. It's also what sours your denomination officials. They've given you money. It's all gone, and you need more. We will present more on the issue of money in chapter 7.

These Things Must Be Present When You Do an Ultrasound on the "Baby in the Womb"

Every church plant has critical milestones that must show progress twelve to eighteen months after the public launch. If not, it's crisis time:

- the ability to add "significant" numbers to the initial group of people (think in terms of multiples, not addition)
- multiple people groups started around tasks, ministries, and/or relationships
- financial ownership resulting from formal teaching on "stewardship" and a giving plan in place—not the equivalent of financial self-sufficiency, but the first step toward it
- "essential" ministries in place that reflect the needs of the mission field
- spiritual formation opportunities and disciplines offered that produce "disciples," not just church members
- "perceived" progress—in way of size and development—by outside observers
- certainty and stability of leadership (i.e., ministry directors identified and all performing adequate tasks to serve the infrastructure)
- proper adjustments in strategy to reach the mission field

■ ■ ■ SUPERVISORY COMMENTS: Unfortunately, supervisors often succumb to the financial pressure and push for public launch before the plant has sufficient people size. Don't do it! Launching too soon actually increases the church's debt load.

You must give the plant enough gestation time to launch with a critical mass. So, don't pressure your planters to launch or charter or arbitrarily set a launch date. The date must take into account the need for "critical mass." Arbitrarily setting a date causes the planter to launch prematurely, the launch team to lose heart, and the church to become an anemic church with insufficient amounts of critical mass and funds for them and for you.

Bottom line: The supervising agency expects some kind of return on its investment, and it never materializes.

● ● ● COACHING COMMENTS: The coach needs to ask, "What is your people-gathering strategy that you're building into the life of the launch team?"

Often the main task of a coach is to freeze-frame the timeline. Church planters often make the mistake of doing the right thing at the wrong time. They become impatient with waiting, and so they launch prematurely. The role of the coach is to say, "Let's slow down until we reach 'critical mass.' What do you think that number would be, and what can you do to reach it *before* launching?"

5

Evangelism Ceases after the Launch

Philip found Nathanael and told him,... "Come and see."

JOHN 1:45–46

Sally had avoided all of the mistakes we have mentioned so far: she had embedded prayer in the DNA of the church, developed a community filled with God's love for people, and launched the church with a critical mass. Everything was rosy, except one thing—Sally and her team believed if they provided the very best worship experience for those attending, people would continue to show up. They became so involved in getting everything ready for the worship event they didn't have the energy or the time to continue inviting their people networks.

Sally and her team also made one other huge mistake. They not only believed more people would continue to show up, they also believed that these new people would automatically pitch in with their time and money. Not so. It takes time for new people to become vessels through which God can work.

By the third month the launch team was worn out, and worn out people aren't very good ambassadors of good news.

By the second year the leader's passion for inviting people became sidetracked. Sally began directing her messages more to church members instead of guests, and became focused on internal "church" things. Her time spent inviting people and encouraging her leaders to invite people slowly took a backseat to taking care of the "church things" and "church members." More and more of everyone's time was spent on perfecting the charter or constitution, and establishing committees or teams.

It wasn't long before people began complaining that Sally wasn't spending enough time with them. "Don't you love us anymore?" they asked. "Don't you think we should start taking better care of who we've got before going after any more people?" "If we add that second service, we won't know everyone anymore."

Based on Sally's actions, these responses are to be expected. People are riddled with sin. The best of us is selfish, if allowed to get away with it. And that's what Sally did. Her example allowed them to get away with focusing attention on "church" things and themselves instead of doing what they were called to do—make disciples. She ceased role-modeling inviting and caved in to their cries for her to become their caregiver. More and more of her time was spent caring for them instead of appointing people to be the caregivers. Her time was diverted from praying for and being among those outside the church, to becoming a pastor to a small group of people, who increasingly became ingrown.

Pastor, your best defense is a good offense. Your response to ingrown people is crucial. Respond with comments such as, "Isn't the real question, 'Does everyone in town know God?' not, 'Do we all know one another?'" If that doesn't work, show them the door!

During the third year the guests dried up. Before Sally knew it, she was left with an ingrown congregation content with her loving them and nothing more. Inviting the public continued to dwindle until finally Sally realized she wasn't spending any time outside the faith community. And her leaders weren't either. The day soon came when her leaders, who had been snatched out of the unchurched world, no longer knew anyone outside the church. That spells the death of a church plant, and the death of the mission.

Evangelism is NOT a "phase" of church life; it's the "LIFE" of the church!

Sally made one fatal mistake—thinking evangelism is just a phase a church goes through on its way to maturity. Evangelism must be embedded as part of the DNA of the plant for it to be successful, much less biblical.

Planter, how much time do you spend in the office and with churched people compared to the time you spend in occupied territory with people who aren't going to church?

One of the hard lessons we learn in consulting with churches is that if the pastor ceases to model inviting the public and pushing the Great Commission then the congregation will become a closed system. An equally hard pill to swallow is that, in the majority of church plants, people are so completely extracted from the culture and spend so much time with church people that over a very short period of time they have no close friends outside the church. Without close relationships outside the church the plant begins to wither.

Too often we've seen a new church developer begin to recruit people and launch the church, and then the people want to turn the new church developer into their personal pastor. The pastor finds it hard to tell them no. But you say, "Surely I'm supposed to love them?" Yes, pastor, you are. But the real act of loving is to grow them into disciples who make other disciples, not to become their personal chaplain.

We know. You feel as if you should take care of them. Not so. Equip some of your people to care for them. That's biblical (Acts 6). Don't let your mercy gift get the best of you and get suckered into feeling guilty. Remember, according to Ephesians 4:11–12 your role is to equip the saints, not take care of them. Your role is to ensure the Great Commandment and the Great Commission are happening in your church.

You must think of your church as a missional outpost, perched on the edge of occupied territory. The missional outpost exists as a community whose primary goal is to live out the Great Commandment in a way that people who are invited into the community experience the love of God in a redeeming way. The Great Commandment bleeds through the community, not in terms of duty, but in the way the followers of Jesus incarnate and communicate who God is.

Evangelism is far more than just Sally and her people inviting people to church. It's the reason the entire community of faith exists. It's the essence of Christian maturity when a Christian reaches out to a stranger with the story of God's love. Making disciples is not about adding people to your church. Making disciples is about introducing people to God's love found within the community of faith. Making disciples is helping people fall in love with God and becoming more like Jesus.

Our experience has confirmed that over 80 percent of those who visit a church and return to that church and gradually become enfolded into that faith community do so on the elbow of someone already connected to that church. So work on making your church the most loving and inviting place in the area so when people do show up they know they are loved.

Pastors, your people have to invite others into the community of faith, and the community has to be an inviting place when they arrive.

Developing a Culture of Inviting

We don't like the "E" word, *evangelism,* because it has so much baggage. It's also a scary issue for most people. We prefer the word *invite.* Even though inviting people is still scary to most people, the word is not nearly as frightening as the word *evangelism.*

The New "E" Word

The new "E" word is *elbow.* Our experience has confirmed that over 80 percent of everyone who visits a church, returns to that church, and gradually becomes enfolded into that faith community, does so on the *elbow* of someone already connected to that church. So what we want is for people to invite their networks to "come and see" what you're doing.

How often do you provide events to which your people can invite their friends to "come and see"?

The old style of planting a church was, "Build it and they will come." Find a piece of land, build a building at an enormous cost, and then, like a doctor, set out your shingle and wait for them to come. That approach doesn't work anymore. We call it the "old wineskin" approach. Many of your leaders may not understand this fact. After most church marketing campaigns, we find many church veterans stunned when people don't show up. They have prepared everything for them and they don't show. "We're doing everything we can. How come they don't come?" Rarely do the planter and launch team make more than an obligatory effort to embed the "inviting" gene into the DNA of the new congregation.

When we meet with launch teams, the laypeople are confused that people don't seem to like what they have to offer. They assume Joe and Sally Doe are driving down the street one Saturday morning and notice the elementary school and the sign that says "Happy Valley Church." "Look, honey, a church. Let's try it tomorrow!" That's still the unspoken expectation of many church people—maybe even your launch team.

You can put on the best dog-and-pony show on earth, but it no longer has the power to pull people from the comfort of their daily routines and place them in chairs in a new church. Evangelism workshops work hard to highlight this change; but at the end of the day, the first question asked is, "What do you think about marketing and advertising?"

What most people don't realize is we have moved from an "attract culture," where "Build it and they will come" works, to an "invite culture," where people are far more likely to show up at church if a friend invites them. Your people are all creatures of an attract culture, and rarely have they ever been part of a church plant, so the chances are they've never been singled out to actually invite someone to an event. Inviting a friend is a foreign concept to them. But that is what they must do.

One of the key tasks of a launch team is coming up with events to which each member of the launch team invites somebody who is not connected to a church. You need to train your people to say to their networks—"We're starting a church for those who are thinking about coming to (or coming back to) church."

Old Wineskins	New Wineskins
Come	Go
Passive	Active
Impersonal	Personal
Old Style	Today's Style
Wait	Connect
Program	Networks

Finding the Right Culture of Inviting

Direct mail campaigns are iffy. For every church that uses mailers and has 200 people show up, 500 churches use mailers and have three people show up. There are just enough of these churches where mailers have worked to tease churches into trying this strategy.

The inviting practice we do know works every time is: the more your leaders invite their networks, the more likely your church is to grow.

You would think networking comes naturally with church planters—not so. We spend an increasing percentage of our time teaching church planters how to network with people—joining the Rotary, riding in police cars, talking with realtors, etc. It's just easier to write a check for some form of mail campaign than to step out on a limb and invite your networks.

Now here's the kicker—to network the planter has to like people and the area. Inviting people to your church is one thing; inviting them to Christ is another. It's a heart thing. To do it, you must like people and be convinced the way you do it is from God.

How Do You Add People?

As the planter, you must keep in mind that, no matter what you do, you are going to be the primary "people adder," especially in the early months and years. If you don't make contact after contact with the public, the likelihood of success is almost zero.

Church planting is a "contact sport."

Although we will say more about this later, here are a few helpful hints:

- Never forget church planting is a "contact sport": everyone must contact all of their networks for it to succeed—family, friends, neighbors, and associates—all the time. They won't make these contacts unless you lead by example and constantly encourage them to do so.

- You need a number of monthly, rather than weekly, events that preview your upcoming church. As soon as you start weekly, you are now having church; and if you only have a few people, that's not critical mass.
- You need to have continual events designed to invite or inform newcomers about what you are doing (not a formal service). Examples: an information meeting where your people invite their friends, or a social event such as a Valentine Dinner dance where your people are encouraged to invite their friends and make relational connections.
- You need to spend 50 percent of your time making contact with the public.

Assimilation

One of the biggest difficulties planters have is they don't talk to enough people. Our suggestion is a planter needs to talk to one thousand people the first year. Most of the conversations need to be one-on-one. You can count on this rule: if you don't talk to people, they won't be in the pews. Everywhere you go, everyone you meet is fair game for these conversations—everyone, everywhere.

What do you do in these conversations?

- Tell your story.
- Let them tell their story.
- Let them ask questions.
- Talk about joining the vision "stuff."

Too many planters spend the first year in their office setting up the "paraphernalia" of the church, such as the office, computers, Web sites, business cards/stationary, legal stuff, and brochures. You really don't need much of this "stuff" in the beginning. Save the money, and focus on meeting and inviting people to join your vision.

Networking and Gathering People

Because so many books address this issue, we're just going to hit the highlights. What follows is enough to get you headlong into the contact sport of church planting.

- Start out by deciding how many people you need for a critical mass and how many you have now you can count on. The difference is your goal.
  You have two primary fields from which to glean people. One is within the Christian community—mission boards, pastors' meetings, info meetings, and church lobbies. Don't be afraid to talk with other churches about "loaning" you some people. The other field is the mission field, which is your primary target.
- Schedule networking time, so that you spend at least 50 percent of your time networking. You might make a list of all the churchy things you are asked to do that keep you from spending this amount of time and begin scratching them off your "to do" list.
- We recommend targeting reaching twenty-five new people each week prior to launch, and five each week after the launch.
- You must overcome internal resistance: "It's not my gift, and it really doesn't match my personality profile." "I'm just too busy. I already have more than I can handle." "I don't have very many opportunities." "I can't stand rejection." "I feel inferior. I need to look like I have it all together." "Networking seems impersonal, forced, and cold." "I don't want to look like a salesman trying to sell something." Either get over these, or get out of church planting.
- Pray that God will send new people your way and keep you ready to respond to them immediately.
- Memorize your opening introduction of yourself to new people. Make sure it is clear, concise, and distinctive. Remember, you are selling yourself, not a vision, or a church.

Keep in mind most good conversations are dialogues rather than monologues, so ask a lot of questions.

The Fix: Avoiding the Mistake

Sally forgot a couple of important things along the way. For one, reaching out and inviting friends and neighbors, much less strangers, to church is counter to our way of life. Even the most committed Christians find it hard to invite their networks. It's not the most comfortable thing for a person to do. What blows our mind is that most Christians have enough nonbelieving friends that they don't have to reach out to strangers. All they need to do is to view their friends through the lens of Christ.

So for a church to continue inviting and welcoming the public, the leader has to keep the pressure on. A pastor can keep the concept of inviting in the forefront of the congregation's consciousness in several ways.

- Make certain that "taste and see" events are planned strategically throughout the life of the congregation (more on these events later).
- Reinforce the Great Commission every time you preach, or have a conversation, or attend a meeting. Never assume that just because you have the best worship in town people will continue to show up. Never let a few needy members take precedence over the needs of the many outside of your church.
- Before the church launches, call on your leaders to spend 50 percent of their time in the contact sport of connecting with new people.
- Once the church launches, as planter, you will want to spend 25 percent of your time connecting with new people.

"Taste and See" Events

"Taste and see" events are comfortable and intentional gatherings designed specifically for your launch team to invite their networks to "come and see" your emerging faith community. As such, these events cause the launch team to behave differently. This is not a passive participation. The goal is for invitees to "encounter" the community you are forming and, by rubbing up against it, to want to proceed further. These events are based on the nature of how the people connect in their place of living. The events come in two sizes: small (4–20 people) and large (50—200 people).

These events are about one thing: putting new people in seats—nothing more. The planter has to guard against the event taking on a church family atmosphere, where outsiders feel marginalized. Using these events to form community within the launch team dampens any enthusiasm for inviting and evangelism.

These events must be "doable" for those who you want to participate. Far too many planters challenge their people to "bring five families." Five is unrealistic. The bar is raised so high people walk away from the idea. So ask each family or individual to bring one person.

It is easy to get "inebriated" on a good idea. Everybody talks about it. Volunteers work hard for it. Then it flops, and everybody is upset. It is better to sober up at the outset and judge the event objectively before doing it.

It's best if you develop established criteria for running any people-gathering event:

- What is its purpose? To gather people! Therefore, people must invite people.
- Is it "doable"?
- Do normal people do this activity, or is it so bizarre they will wonder about you?
- What is the hand-off? A hand-off is a very deliberate and consistent follow-up to each invited attendee at a people-gathering event.

Focusing on these events will begin to change the behavior of the congregation. Replacing "just us" events with "just them" events forces the congregation to think outside itself. So make room for three to five all-church people-gathering events, with some sort of Christmas service being a prime example.

Every time we see a new church plant start with a bang and fall apart a couple of years later, we know somewhere along the way running the church took precedence over inviting people to Jesus and to the church. You can avoid this mistake by making the Great Commission indispensable to the DNA of your church.

Sally forgot what the church community is all about: making new converts, not running the church. The church itself should never be the object of affection—making disciples should be the focus. Church people come with so much baggage concerning the church. They act as if the church exists solely for those who are part of it. That's why we think the best metaphor for a church is a "missionary outpost" whose mission is to invade and infect occupied territory with the good news, and from that develop a community whose purpose in life is to continue changing the area around them. The *ecclesia,* the "called-out ones," don't remain aloof and distant from the mission field. They penetrate it, navigating in such a way as to invite people into community. This continual "going out" and "inviting in" results in new converts being sent back out to invite *their* networks into the community, and then sending them back out, and so on, and so on.

When the launch team begins to practice the DNA of inviting people before the launch and to experience the joy of seeing their invitees respond, they will more likely continue this behavior after the launch. Only a few will get caught up in running the church or in seeing disciple-making as merely spiritual formation. Instead, they will understand that, along with community, the role of the church is to change the world, or at least their city.

Connectors

A new plant needs two types of folks working the crowd before and after the services: connectors and greeters. Connectors are different from greeters. Greeters are stationary; connectors walk around. The goal of the connectors is to connect people to one another so they find community and return for a second visit. Connectors do provide information, but that is not the goal. You only need one to three connectors in a new church. Here are the key aspects of the connector's role:

- They have the gift of hospitality, very warm and welcoming.
- They greet all people, but focus on new people.

Connectors ask two questions:

- "You've probably been attending for some time, but I have not yet met you."
- "How did you hear about the church?"

Based on these responses, connectors connect people to one or two people on their first visit who may share similar characteristics or interests. Connectors may offer to sit with guests during the service if it seems appropriate. After the event, they document the information they have gathered and combine it with anything that might be on the registration sheets.

■ ■ ■ SUPERVISORY COMMENTS: Continually remind the planter that the goal is new converts, not just numbers in the pew. Even though putting people in the pews is important, real evangelism is helping non-Christians enter a relationship with Jesus Christ.

Also, remember you're not just funding the conception and birth of the new church. You must maintain a supervisory type relationship with them all the way to maturity. And maturity comes when they birth another church, go multiple-site, or add a second worship service. So we don't recommend giving the planter all of the money upfront. We've seen too many mismanage the money in the early going and wind up without enough money to get the project into orbit.

We would prefer you meet with the group and pledge all the money to the project, but only "grant" the first round, usually 30–50 percent of the total. Place the rest of the money in "escrow." This first round of funding is considered "seed" money to launch the church. So, while pledging it all, the supervisor only grants a certain amount, in good faith, believing that the amount is sufficient to get the project launched and under way.

Then, somewhere near the timeframe for the second round, usually eighteen to twenty-four months out, the "escrowed" funds will be released to the project team. However, this release of funds is not guaranteed. It must be earned.

This funding process should be explained to the planter and team before the project starts. At that time, the supervisor will want to meet with the planter, designated representatives from the groups involved, the coach, and other important people for a discussion around the "benchmarks" that will need to be in place to receive the second round of funding.

The "benchmarks" must meet criteria that demonstrate progress. For example, if the church had eight small groups in place at launch, it should have at least doubled the number of small groups and the people in them. A bad example would be, "Our people are growing in their faith." While this may be true, the only way to measure such a thing is to look at the spiritual disciplines of those people, along patterns of increased financial giving and habits of Bible reading, etc. One is too subjective, the other quite evident.

● ● ● COACHING COMMENTS: Ask your planter for a schedule of how time is spent. Before the launch make sure the planter spending 50 percent of the time connecting with new people. Twelve weeks after launch, ask the planter to provide another schedule. A quick look will indicate what has become of connecting with new people. Remember, the goal is new converts more than just shuffling sheep from one church to another.

A good way to measure "growth after launch" is:

- Ask the planter to count the number of adults (post-high-school age and older) attending each service.
- After the first ten weeks of public worship, throw out the high attendance number and low attendance number.
- Divide by eight. This number will yield a "baseline" from which to evaluate numerical growth and progress in the future. A reasonable expectation in areas experiencing new or transition growth is the "baseline" should increase by three to four times within the first twenty-four to thirty months.
- If, after twelve to eighteen months of public ministry, the "baseline" has increased by only 10 percent, this indicates a glaring problem and should be addressed immediately. The coach has to pose these questions to the planter and team on a continuous basis:

    — What is your continuing outreach?
    — What is your continual strategy to invite new people into the mix?
    — In the past quarter, how many new people have visited the church attached to the "elbow" of someone already in the church?

6

No Plan for the Other Six Days of the Week

And He gave some as apostles, and some as prophets, and some as evangelists, and some as pastors and teachers, for the equipping of the saints for the work of service.

EPHESIANS 4:11–13, NAB

Robert was a great recruiter. As a result, 300 people showed up opening day. Robert and the launch team were ecstatic over the turnout. Not only that, everything went like clockwork during the grand opening—the parking team, the nursery, the children's area, and the worship. Even the technical pieces during worship went off without a hitch.

Pastors are so fixated on the main event they give no thought to what to do with the people who show up.

Robert and his team met that evening for a private celebration to thank God for the morning and to encourage one another.

Then it dawned on the group: "What are we going to do with these people tomorrow? How are we going to connect them to our fledgling new community, to each other, and to God?"

Before the launch, most planters spend a great deal of time designing the "style" of the main gathering event, whether it is in a home, an auditorium, or a sanctuary. Because style of music and liturgy seems paramount, the planter thinks of little else. Consequently, what to do with people once they attend, let alone how to help them move further into the faith community, is reduced to an afterthought.

Prior to the launch a plan must be in place to connect people to each other and to God. Failing to do this results in a church dependent on the planter.

Churches that plateau at 150 participants lean heavily, and almost exclusively, on the "corporate" event of public worship. They fail to develop a process to connect people to each other and to God throughout the week. Neither do they have a plan to orient attendees to the mission of the new church. It's just, "Come to the show," with little thought given to the relational aspects of developing the spiritual community. Many planters are so good at recruiting and designing that people attending are attracted to them and to the show. The longer this continues the more everyone depends on a personal relationship with the pastor and the Sunday morning service. This is especially true of churches with a "sacramental" tradition.

The lack of a plan after launch exposes shallow thinking in several areas:

- Mature Christians have no place to exercise their relational gifts.
- Christ is compartmentalized to a few hours every week.
- Little thought is given to how to disciple the people who show up and want to move deeper into their understanding of the gospel.

- "Church" is an event, rather than a community.
- No clear pattern exists for people to connect relationally, except with the pastor.
- Leaders think biblical discipleship has been accomplished.

New churches must put systems in place for Monday through Friday, moving people further into contact with the emerging faith community. Through some means, the church must develop a "relational" culture.

The Hairball Model of Church Planting

Ever seen a really big hairball? The hair becomes so tightly wound it almost looks as if it is one solid piece of hair. In fact, the horn on a rhinoceros is nothing more than one tightly wound hairball. That's what happens to a church where there's no plan to hand off people during the week. Everything, and everyone, is tightly wound around the pastor. The hairball model is a classic codependent model of leadership, or, we should say, *lack* of leadership. Because no one is ever handed-off to someone else, everyone becomes accustomed to having a close relationship with the pastor and depending on him or her for everything. As a result, everyone competes for the pastor's attention. The hairball model is nothing more than a church of 130 people who function like one gigantic small group, with the pastor as the small group leader. Everybody knows everybody. It's large, but it's still manageable, because it's one big happy family.

For the church to grow, the point person has to hand people off and connect them to other shepherds rather than stay personally attached to them. In the early stages especially, the planter cannot afford to get too "attached" to anyone.

What's Wrong with This Picture?

Several things are wrong with this picture. The seeds are

sown for the people to become dependent on the pastor for everything, and for the church to plateau at around 130.

Studies show that an effective person seldom has more than sixty to ninety adult relationships. Add a few dozen kids, and you have the typical American church. Get the picture? If everyone is dependent on the pastor, the church plateaus at around 130 because people have to be connected to the church or they leave. Sure, some super pastors can take a church to 200 or 300 all by themselves. We've seen that happen. We've also seen these pastors wind up locked in their closet in a fetal position because of the burden of so many people.

The planter must have a plan for moving people into community without having to be the sole relational component; otherwise, the church remains weak and small.

But that's not all. Dependence on the pastor turns the church inward instead of keeping its focus on reaching out. Everyone knows that the addition of more people threatens this great relationship with the pastor and creates competition between parishioners for the pastor's time.

But here's the kicker most planters don't realize. When a pastor goes off to an evangelism seminar or church growth seminar and comes back to his or her large, small group and says, "We need to implement the Great Commission and grow," they hear, "*My* pastor doesn't love *me* anymore. *My* pastor will be spending less time with *me*." So they dig in with passive-aggressive behavior. They don't invite their networks anymore because more people means, "*I've* got to share *my* pastor, and I kind of like the way I've got it right now."

Most of your leaders aren't against evangelism or growing the church; they're against sharing you with others. Whose fault is it? Yours, because you didn't have a plan in place before you planted to equip them and hand them off to other leaders.

But the problem doesn't end here. What if the Sunday show is so good that people continue to visit because of the buzz it's created in the area? Guess what happens? Because everyone is tied to the pastor, the church does not have room for any more relationships; and the church becomes a revolving door.

We're not through. The problem gets much worse.

The codependent model doesn't connect people with God. It connects them with the pastor. The pastor is mediating the relationship. Is that what you want?

Let's go even deeper with this problem. Dependence on the pastor keeps your people from reaching their potential in Christ. They can go only as far in their relationships with God and one another as the pastor goes. Is that what you want? All good parents hope their children have a better life than they have, right? Well the hairball model never lets your people outgrow you.

Thought we were through with this problem? Wrong. There's more.

When the pastor leaves for another church, a giant sucking sound takes place. No one knows what to do or how to keep the church together. That's one of the main reasons the average church plant begins to decline the fourth or fifth year—the founding pastor leaves, and that means the relational hub holding the people together also leaves.

But there's even more wrong with this picture. Because of the dependence on the planter, the people aren't connected to each other.

So you have to have a plan in place in which people are handed off to other leaders to minister in all areas of the church. If you don't, the hairball gets thicker and thicker until it's too hard for new people to break into the group. Your people will have their basic relationship with you, and biblical ministry is over.

So what are the telltale signs of a pastor who isn't handing-off the people and is hording all the ministry?

- You don't have a plan for moving people into community without you having to be the sole relational component.

- You spend all of your time on the Sunday event.
- You do all of the teaching.
- You've been teaching a Bible class your entire tenure with no thought of finding your replacement.
- You do all the normal pastoral ministry.
- You're in the office much of the day.
- You're not training someone to take your place in some ministry.
- You don't pray for God to send more people your way who can do ministry better than you can.
- You go out of your way to avoid conflict, especially if it requires you to fire a paid staff person or replace a volunteer.
- You've been leading the same small group from the beginning and haven't figured out how to multiply it into two or more small groups.
- In your small group you allow the people to default to you for all the answers.
- You don't have a list of people you are equipping to take responsibility for ministry or for other groups. I (Bill) call this your "to be" list.

The 125 Ceiling

Most everyone has heard of the "200 in worship" or the 125-member ceiling. The concept is that the vast majority of churches never grow beyond 125 members.

This ceiling is in place because the majority of pastors behave like codependents, rather than responsible shepherds, and don't develop a plan for handing-off people to other relational connections. This is nothing other than a large small group, with the pastor functioning as the leader of a small group. This behavior creates an organizational model that relies on the ability of the pastor to maintain relationships with about ninety adults, which, in turn, keeps the church small.

Instead of equipping and handing-off people, these pastors try to break through the ceiling by creating ways to create more room for more people. We've seen them try it two ways. One way is to add more space by adding a worship service or a larger sanctuary. However, that fails to render the results expected because everyone is still dependent on the pastor. The other way is to actually lose people. That's right. They allow people to come and go. It's been our experience that when a codependent grows a church to 150, over the next couple of years he or she will grow it back down toward 100.

Let me (Jim) tell you a story of a very effective pastor who unfortunately began to behave as a chaplain. Due to the massive people influx in his mission field, his church grew from 300 to 800. Because he lacked the capacity to manage that many relationships and failed to come up with a plan to equip and hand off, he chose to leave. The pastor who replaced him had had a quite similar DNA—very strong at nurturing, with little in the way of administrative gifts. However, this pastor had acquired the "multiplication gene" somewhere along the way, and had a plan to hand off the care and feeding to others. In less than two years, that same church increased to 2,000.

The 15 percent of pastors with the right DNA get past the 200 barrier with no little to any training. They just do what's natural to them. On the other hand, those shepherds possessing the "codependent gene," find that growing a church beyond a large small group goes against their nature. They don't have the capacity to hand off people into the care of others, or to fire people, or to show the door to volunteers who either challenge their spiritual authority, or try to change the DNA of the church, or cause it harm.

The plan for the other six days is counterintuitive to a natural codependent instinct.

Discipleship Is a Trade, Not a Course

Discipleship is not something you learn. A disciple is someone you become. Many pastors think of discipleship as a course to be taught, so they gather people and begin taking people through a course of study. This is not good. First, discipleship is more on-the-job training; and second, courses keep your people at church rather than connecting with new people.

Jim had an experience in his last church plant that explains the difference between teaching a course and offering on-the-job discipling. Before he launched his last church, he recruited some men to join him in some "prayer rides." Instead of having them meet at his house to pray for the city, Jim piled them into a van and carted them to a high bluff just outside Denver that overlooked their mission field. He had them exit the van and pointed out the many lights emanating from the houses in their mission field. "These are the people God has charged us to reach." He directed the men to kneel and pray for the city with no other instructions. He noted that most of the men had difficulty even stuttering out a generic prayer. They gathered into the van and proceeded to another high location and prayed again. The third location was the parking lot of the local high school. Once again they knelt, on asphalt this time, and prayed. For several weeks, this band of brothers followed this ritual. On one of those occasions, Jim noticed a change in the men. Their prayers remained quite simple, but their demeanor was one of sobbing and weeping.

Every one of these men was a veteran of churches and small group Bible studies, and church boards. They'd heard countless teachings and sermons on prayer, but they had seldom prayed. They'd heard countless sermons on having a "burden" for those outside of Christ, but cognitive discussions do little to break the heart. The simple act of getting out into the mission field and "seeing" it resulted in transformed hearts.

The Fix: Avoiding the Mistake

It should be clear by now that a healthy church plant has a clearly defined process for handing-off people who come to the church so only a handful of people are personally connected to the pastor. In the beginning it is the launch team. These relationships may change over time, or they may remain the primary relationships. But one thing is constant: the pastor and all staff, paid and unpaid, understand that the role of leadership is to equip and hand off to others. And this is their primary role in ministry.

There's nothing wrong with a church of 130 as long as it's exhibiting biblical fruits where the pastor is handing off ministry. However, it borderlines on immoral for a pastor to horde all the ministry and keep the church from experiencing the joy of being in ministry together.

So, if you have a church of 150 people, take 50 of them and hand them off to a shepherd you've trained and trust. You'll find it doesn't take a whole lot for him or her to take those people and in two years turn them into 150. Even a codependent can do that, because codependents want to reach out. They just don't want to go beyond their own relational capacity.

Because it's so hard for most pastors to hand off people to minister or be ministered to, some suggestions might help:

- The capacity for care is somewhere between ten and fifteen, so you have to develop a plan for breaking through that ceiling without you doing it.
- If you want people to grow and/or receive the best care possible, you must equip other shepherds and hand people off to them.
- When the church is small, the goal of all equipping is to work yourself out of a job. The smaller the church the more time you need to spend equipping and training a few key leaders to take responsibility for ministry. In the early years, I (Bill) took people with me to the hospital to let them watch what I did. Then I let them do a little, and in time I let them take over the hospital visits. Don't pastor as if you are responsible for the entire church. Instead spend most of your time with your ministry directors, paid or unpaid, training them to be able to shepherd a group of people on their own.
- Invest your time in people you think are able to give

leadership to an area of ministry or shepherd a group of people, and avoid spending time with the naysayers or people you discern just want to be spiritually coddled.

- Spend most of your time with people who you feel can either bring other people to the church or lead other people to Christ.

- Develop a small group ministry focused on personal development. It's rare to find a thriving church plant without small groups that grow. For that to happen, the pastor has to role model equipping shepherds and handing them off to shepherd their groups. In the first couple years, particularly in the first year, you hope you're handing leadership off to people who are somewhat healthy. Don't worry too much about whether they know the Bible. You can give them teaching videos to use in their groups. The key is you hand off to people who love Jesus and people and who can lead a group to share life together.[1]

■ ■ ■ SUPERVISORY COMMENTS: Supervisors, after the church launches and begins to grow and the newness wears off, don't be surprised if some of the original people don't begin calling your office to complain about not having access to the pastor anymore. The calls come from those people who no longer feel "connected" to their pastor, or their pastor no longer has time for them. You must not give in to these kind of complaints. You must understand that those planters with the apostolic gene will not revert to a shepherding role. But those planters with the shepherding gene will too quickly revert to

---

[1]Some of the best books on small groups that multiply are Bill Easum and John Atkinson, *Go Big with Small Groups* (Nashville: Abingdon Press, 2006); M. Scott Boren, *Making Cell Groups Work* (Houston: Cell Group Resources, 2003); Neil Cole, *The Organic Church* (San Francisco: Jossey-Bass, 2005); Joel Comiskey, *How to Be a Great Cell Group Coach* (Houston: Cell Group Resources, 2003); Steve Cordle, *The Church in Many Houses* (Nashville: Abingdon Press, 2005); Carl George, *Prepare Your Church for the Future* (Tarrytown, N.Y.: F. H. Revell, 1991); Joe Myers, *The Search to Belong* (Grand Rapids: Youth Specialties, 2003); Ralph W. Neighbour Jr., *Where Do We Go from Here?* (Houston: Touch Publications, 1990); Wolfgang Simson, *Houses that Change the World* (Waynesboro, Ga.: Authentic Lifestyle, 2003).

taking care of people and will lose any incentive to reach more people and the church will plateau, typically within two years of launch.

You have the responsibility, prior to commissioning the planter, to make certain the planter has thought through a "hand-off" plan for relational support and spiritual formation of those attending.

One of the critical "benchmarks" in evaluating progress lies in the development of relational groups that don't include the planter's presence. If groups are not increasing with regularity, trouble lies ahead.

● ● ● COACHING COMMENTS: A good coach wants to know if the people are connected just to the planter, or are they going to be handed-off? Most effective church planters are good at recruiting people, but find it hard to equip people and hand them off so they are no longer connected to them. So you must ask the planter, "What is your plan for handing off people and getting them connected relationally without everything revolving around you?" Or, "How many people have you handed off this month?" A good example of a helpful suggestion in this area is to tell planters that they can launch a Bible study, but after four to six weeks they need to be gone from the group so they can launch another small group.

7

Fear of Talking about Money until It Is Too Late

"For which of you, when he wants to build a tower, does not first sit down and calculate the cost, to see if he has enough to complete it? Otherwise, when he has laid a foundation, and is not able to finish, all who observe it begin to ridicule him, saying, 'This man began to build and was not able to finish.'"

LUKE 14:28–30, NASB

Terry's church plant was doing well. She'd done her homework—recruiting launch team members, finding good music leaders, connecting people into relational small groups, developing good publicity, a great facility, and, more importantly, she'd raised a lot of money to pay for all these things. Terry was so excited to receive such funding from "angel investors/virtue capitalists" that she splurged a little on the advertising.

So, with ample money and great fanfare, the new venture soared, eclipsing the dreaded "200" barrier and seeing the children's ministry explode. To accommodate the swelling

73

numbers, Terry and her advisors decided to add another service, and complementary children's ministries and childcare at both services. All this required additional rent and school custodian fees. With the expansion of children's ministry, members working in the nursery were drafted to teach, requiring Terry and her team to hire childcare workers.

People continued to invite their networks, and follow-up systems adequately connected people to the discipleship and ministry portions of the still-expanding church. However, the additional people severely taxed those unpaid staff who could manage three to five hours per week, but were now being asked to double and triple their time commitment. Terry knew they couldn't continue to demand this amount of time for long, so she tried to determine which staff needed to be compensated financially for their efforts. This resulted in hiring several part-time paid staff.

A few months into the new format, Terry received a phone call from the person in charge of finances. "Terry, I wanted to alert you to the fact we're running low on money. We received our last check from our sponsors and without that check our income next quarter will fall short of our expenses. With current giving patterns, I estimate we have three to four months before we will not be able to make the rent and pay salaries. What's your plan?"

In the venture capital business of start ups, Terry and her team were about to experience the financial equivalent of a "perfect storm"—diminished cash flow, little or no capital for expansion, and inattention to the management of finances.

In her attention to people and ministry expansion, Terry had ignored the finances and, even now, didn't have a clue as to how to solve it.

The more a new church succeeds, the more likely it runs the risk of financial shortfalls: GROWTH HAS A BIG APPETITE—IT DEMANDS TO BE FED!

"Well," Terry wondered, "What about all the new people now attending? Aren't they giving? One of the reasons my supervisor urged me to start was so the new attendees could start supporting the project." Her treasurer's response gave her little comfort. "Pastor, it appears we have lots of 'tippers,' but very few 'tithers.'"

Most people just coming back to church don't tithe; they tip!

Her next question was, "What about our outside supporters who pledged monthly amounts?" The treasurer explained that, due to the sporadic nature of monthly pledges, these could not be counted on as "monthly" income. More significantly, Terry had not followed up with these "friends of the mission"; and once original obligations had ceased, most supporters redirected their gifts to other projects.

Exasperated, Terry asked the unpaid treasurer, "Who's been keeping track of all this?" to which the man replied, "Pastor, I can help with the collections, deposits, and writing checks; but I don't have the time to do much else."

In his book *Innovation and Entrepreneurship,* Peter Drucker says, "The more successful a new venture, the more dangerous the lack of financial foresight.[1]

Successful new church starts often suffer serious damage, not from an inadequate launch, but from not considering the amount of money needed to sustain the expansion. Most new churches experience a period of time between the launch and the *time when the collections are able to cover all the bills.* This period of time, if too long, no matter how successful the launch, will severely burden the new church to the point of collapse. It may not go out of existence, but the members of the new start find themselves wading in red ink.

---

[1] Peter Drucker, *Innovation and Entrepreneurship* (New York: Harper & Row, 1985), 193.

Undaunted, Terry had one more trick up her sleeve. "We'll apply for more money from our sponsoring agency. Surely our success will prove to them if they give us more, we will get larger." Even at this point, she couldn't see that this would simply hasten the flow of money out the door and cause an even bigger cash flow problem. Besides, the new church was now much larger than many of the existing churches in her tribe, and many on the sponsoring board would have a hard time giving more money to a church that was three or four times larger than the church they attended. The lack of response to her grant application made her bitter. Now she found herself managing two emotions instead of just one.

A quickly called meeting of her brain trust produced the idea of appealing to the congregation to makeup the shortfall. But Terry vigorously opposed this course of action. She explained that she'd read or heard somewhere that such pleas were one of the major reasons unchurched people didn't attend church.

The real Catch-22 is, while new churches can enter financial crisis quickly, extricating themselves from the problem is not so easy. This chapter will give you a framework for addressing money issues before they become serious.

Terry made two devastating mistakes: she had underestimated the cost of growing the church to viability, and she had avoided asking people for money. Even during worship, giving was downplayed. She believed that in time people would give naturally. Was she wrong? Yes! Now she was faced with having to cut back and let some crucial staff go. Instead of progress, it was time to retreat.

So Terry did something she swore she'd never do: she blinked and began to talk privately to certain members of the launch team about the looming financial crisis. Subconsciously she worked the issue into her sermons. What began as routine updates soon became "concerns," which then turned into sporadic "pleas." It left her growing congregation somewhat confused and some even felt duped.

Like many of her colleagues, Terry avoided saying much about money, either from the pulpit, in private conversations, or in membership training. The result was her very successful plant was on the verge of collapse.

One of the worst perpetuated myths is that unchurched people stay away from the church because it is always asking for money. There is no evidence, except anecdotal, to suggest this myth has any relation to reality.

We've yet to see a church plant fail because of lack of funding. What we do see are church planters who do one or several of the following:

- Create unnecessary financial crises by failing to talk about money
- Dangerously dilute the gospel that calls for Christ's followers to place all of themselves under the authority of God
- Greatly underestimate the cost of growing the church to where it has a positive bottom line void of subsidies
- Display grossly inadequate money management skills
- Have a cavalier approach toward discussions about money, bordering on arrogance, suggesting God's blessing of finances is a guarantee
- Do not understand the meaning of "cash flow"
- Wrongly assume that most problems can be solved by more money;
- In their zeal to be "cutting edge," find themselves at odds with Jesus' teaching on discipleship by failing to focus on teaching stewardship from day one.

Growth Has to Be Fed

Often, planters start their campaign to plant a church by committing one of the "unpardonable sins" of church planting—failure to calculate the financial cost during the start-up phase of the work. I don't use the word *unpardonable* lightly, because this is one mistake from which most church plants cannot recover.

They raise just enough money to "give birth" to the plant and create a splash on the scene. However, once the plant is launched, the lack of financial reserve and thinking through cash flow poses a great threat to most new plants' survival.

Naively, both planter and supervisor reason that "once the church gets up and running, we can take an offering and begin to offset our expenses." But once the new church launches, additional expenses escalate to a weekly calendar: facility rental, childcare, printing costs, meetings, advertising, and mailings.

Ironically, the more success the young church has, the more at risk financially they put themselves. Unfortunately, many planters mistakenly believe an increase in attendance will result in as increase in cash flow. Experience teaches just the opposite: more people actually increase the cash drain, thus accelerating the demise of the church. A new church that goes from twenty-five to two hundred and fifty in less than a year most likely will find itself operating more deeply in the red. The causes for the downfall are usually the same: lack of cash to pay the current bills, inability to raise the capital necessary for expansion, and loss of financial control with expenditures.

The bottom line is: Growth has to be fed…with money, and many church planters severely underestimate the financial appetite a growing church possesses. To compound the problem, they see the lack of money as a "faith" issue. In most instances, it's simpler than that. It's a lack of "counting the cost" issue. Failure to foresee this is lack of responsibility on the part of the planter.

The best way to address this financial crisis is to admit you did not adequately count the cost and ask for help.

Oftentimes, financial shortfalls occur at the most critical phase of the new church—accommodating increasing crowds. Caught shorthanded, now the leadership must divert their focus and time and energy to raising money. By the time things settle down and focus is achieved once again, momentum is lost and opportunities squandered.

Planters, as well as judicatories, are notorious for underestimating how much it will cost to plant the church. What they really don't understand is that, the more successful the plant is, the more money it requires. The faster it grows, the more likely you are to go from hand to mouth. You need more room, more staff, more of everything; and all of that costs money. If stewardship of possessions isn't part of the beginning package, any talk about money will bite you in the butt.

Stewardship of money must be taught from the moment you begin to gather people.

Raising "Virtue" Capital

Successful entrepreneurs know that a start up needs all the venture capital it can raise before starting the project. The same is true with planting a church. It always takes a lot more money than is expected. We call this money "virtue capital."

When asked about money, the planter should always reply, "We need MORE."

However, both judicatories and planters fall victim to the concept that the growth of new people will equate into the money needed to keep the plant viable. What they fail to realize is that the giving from new and returning Christians doesn't track with the rise in attendance and the subsequent rise in expenses. So, as attendance goes up, all of the other costs increase geometrically. Any kind of rapid growth lengthens the distance between the funds needed to be viable and the actual amount of money on hand. The church falls farther into the red with each passing week. According to nonprofit guru Peter Drucker, there's an old banker's rule of thumb that assumes bills will come sixty days earlier than expected and receivables will arrive sixty days later than expected.[2]

So effective church planters are learning that a successful church birth and subsequent growth and health demand their attention to raise "virtue capital."

Virtue capital is "sunny day" money.

When a business wants to launch a new product, it goes to investors and asks them to invest. Such investors are called "venture capitalists." Similarly, a new start needs "virtue capital," funds given by people outside the project for the purposes of funding the start up phase *until the regular offering can sustain the work.*

Successful church planters know a gap exists between what they have and what they will need, and so they calculate a realistic "burn rate" of the money and raise "virtue capital." Borrowing from Drucker's analogy of the banker's rule, a new church plant will want to spend some time anticipating its needs for the first three years and raise its "virtue capital" accordingly. With this much lead time, it's almost always possible to finance ministry expansion with cash.

We need to make a distinction here. We're not talking about stewardship of money, which is a subject addressed primarily to disciples. Virtue capital is addressed to investors—anybody in the planter's world, regardless of their religious outlook. These are people who are investing not in the *vision*, but in the *person*. Discipleship is a heart issue; virtue capital is a money issue.

---

[2]Ibid.

Planters need at least two streams of money: one is the monthly income that comes from teaching stewardship to the believers, and one is from the investors outside the church who give sporadically.

Build in the "God Factor"

It's the rare entrepreneurial church planter who calculates accurately the three-year costs in advance, so here's a formula that's proven helpful:

- Write down the amount anticipated to operate the church financially for the first three years.
- Multiply that number by 3.85.
- Experience has shown that the second number will more closely reflect the actual amount needed.

My (Jim's) experience is that the first number reflects what can be accomplished within the existing people network without any assistance from God. As the spiritual leader of the young church, the planter must guard against inadvertently removing God from the equation. The second number builds in the "God Factor" of growth, an essential component to the church's success.

Building in the "God Factor" has other upsides, the most immediate of which is the reintroduction of God into the everyday life of the congregation. In light of this, I encourage planters to give specific financial requests to their intercessory prayer partners and pray God will add to the equation. You want your leaders to look for God's hand in everything they do.

Leverage Your Launch Team

Often the supervisory agency is the only entity invested in the church plant. When this is the case, the odds of the church plant failing are greatly increased. The more investors in the church plant the more likely it is to succeed. So ask your launch team to assist in the raising of virtue capital by contacting their networks.

The first four churches I (Jim) started, I sent letters out to many people who knew me, asking for money. By the fifth church plant, I finally realized I had a hundred adults sitting in my lauunch team meetings, and we hadn't even launched yet! Why couldn't they write their networks? They had friends, relatives, neighbors, and business associates they could ask to support this new venture. So I put together a form letter and asked them to send it to their networks. It was late October. And guess what? More than $40,000.00 came in. From then on we followed that plan every year.

Sample Fund Raising Letter

Dear Members and Friends of Church of the Holy Spirit,

We're excited about what God has done at Church of the Holy Spirit in just a few short months. We have seen changed lives and experienced significant numerical growth. Our children's programs are becoming full, and we are adding rooms to expand them. The need for a youth minister is critical. Our home groups are expanding and drawing in others. The thought of adding another service is ever on our minds.

Due to the expansion of the ministry so quickly, I'm writing to ask you to consider making an end of the year financial gift to the ministry of the Church of the Holy Spirit. This will cover many of the start up costs associated with a new ministry venture. Please consider your gift as "*virtue* capital."

Please prayerfully consider the enclosed card and return it by _____.

Thanks so much for considering your partnership in Church of the Holy Spirit.

You see, planter, like everything else, you're not the only fundraiser in the church. Encourage your launch team to participate in the raising of virtue capital.

Disciple Rather than Beg

Too many planters have bought into the "myth" that unchurched people don't attend church "because they're always talking about money." In all our interviews we've never heard any unchurched person say they failed to attend or return due to the issue of money. The complaint "the church is always talking about money" owes its origins to a vocal group of "church people" who many years ago didn't agree with some financial decision in their church and yanked their pledge, putting the church in financial jeopardy. Only then did they become tired of hearing the leadership plead for money.

However, we must realize there is a difference between making last-minute, emotional pleas for money from the pulpit and teaching good stewardship of money.

Bill Hybels talks about the number one thing that turns people off being talking about money.[3] What they don't understand is he isn't talking against teaching good stewardship; he is referring to those emotional appeals from the pulpit. That's what turns people off. Some of our (Jim and Bill) biggest givers have been previously unchurched people. If you introduce them to the full gospel, it won't turn them off; it will take them deeper into their relationship with God. You don't lead with the subject of money, but you don't avoid it either.

Most church planters, if they would just draw up a simple plan, could avoid most of the problems associated with this mistake. We suggest you make up a weekly "disclaimer" about finances and giving and use it verbatim. Making a disclaimer during the time of collection can actually be a "teaching moment" to all attending. Here is what you should say.

---

[3]Church Leadership Institute lectures.

We've come to that time in our service when we collect
the financial offerings. For those of you who are visiting
with us, please feel no obligation. But for those of you
who call _____ your church home, your financial commitment is very important to sustaining this ministry.

Jesus placed a direct connection between one's treasures
and one's heart—"For where your treasure is, there your heart
will be also" (Mt. 6:21). We've seen many planters fail because
they don't understand this and don't teach it to their leaders.
Ironically, many of the mainline planters who focus on social
justice issues also miss this connection.

Teaching stewardship of money is a principle of discipleship;
it's not a membership issue. How a person handles money is a
clear barometer of the person's spirituality. It's imperative we
preach the whole gospel.

Avoid Crises Fund-Raising

Even if a new church is doing well, raising cash in a hurry
and in a "crisis" is never easy and always expensive. It may not
cost more money to raise cash in a crisis, but it will cost the
leader a certain amount of credibility, often leading to a crisis
of confidence. You can do this once or twice; but if it becomes
a way of life, leaders lose confidence in the planter's ability to
plan ahead.

Wasting Money

Not all church plants are short on money. Some have more
than they need, and they still fail because they do not use the
money wisely. We've seen church planters waste the majority
of their start up money on what we call the "paraphernalia" of
church planting: office location, extravagant Web sites, stationery
and business cards, and brochures. Not using money wisely will
cost you major dollars in unrealized funding and support.

I (Jim) once conducted an autopsy of a failed church plant,
where the planter had spent the first eight months finding a

strategically located office; outfitting the office with computers, copiers, furniture, and stationery; hiring an office assistant; having a brochure designed; and getting a Web site operational. How many do you think the planter had on her launch team? Five! And these five occupied all the planter's time, effectively turning her into a chaplain, not an apostle. When the church plant closed, it still had money in the bank!

Often the problem with money is that the planter burns through it without a strategic plan for its use.

We've talked with many regular attendees in church plants who are humble, wealthy, benevolent people. They're just not benevolent to their church plant because most church planters are terrible managers of money. They may know how to raise money, but they misuse it and seldom understand cash flow. People who have a lot of money usually are very particular with how they let go of it, and they're very happy to give it to people they know will make good use of it. But seeing it handled in a cavalier fashion doesn't build confidence.

For this reason, we don't recommend planters have total control on how they spend the money. However, the problem is many supervisors or oversight committees don't have a clue how to advise the planter on spending the money. They also have don't have a clear, set oversight procedure of how money is to be handled._Still, someone who understands how to spend the money needs to oversee the process. Some processes should be set in place to monitor the flow of money to guard against impulsive spending:

- Have the planter's bank send a copy of the monthly bank statement to the treasurer of the sponsoring agency.
- Require any purchases above a certain amount to get a second look.

While many perceive this as heavy-handed, it's been our experience it will alleviate many hurt feelings down the road.

Some Money Basics

Some planters don't know how to talk about money, and some actually believe if you don't talk about it God will provide. Neither reason for keeping mum about money works. You have to talk about stewardship of life from the beginning, and that includes money. Many on the launch team should be tithers by the time you launch.

Take an Offering Every Service

Every church plant should take an offering from the very beginning. Baskets in the back of the room don't cut it. They send the wrong message to the person looking for a serious place to give their money. Baskets in the rear scream, "The way we handle money isn't important." Putting baskets in the back doesn't teach people how to handle their money. If you want serious givers to give to your plant, take an offering; and don't use baskets in the back of the room.

Know What Everyone Gives

Planters should know how much people have pledged to the project and what they are actually giving. Planters also have the responsibility to identify those who have the gift of giving so that they can disciple them according to their gift.

A rule needs to be heard here—"No pay, no play." If a person isn't financially invested in your church plant, one of four things always happens: one, they try to monopolize your time; two, they become constant complainers; three, they create the impression that they're just "one good sermon away" from pledging; or four, they disappear. In any case, these are not the people you need on your launch team or leadership circle. They are not the people with whom you spend most of your discipling time.

We know this recommendation is controversial. We also know that not knowing what people give makes it impossible for the planter to be strategic in both spending time and selecting leadership. God will not honor leaders who are not giving according to their means, and if the planter doesn't know what people are giving, the planter has no way to ensure the church has the right leadership.

We're not talking about giving special attention to big givers. We're talking about the planter investing in people who are invested in the Gospel. There's a difference. Everyone needs someone to minister to them; but not everyone should be ministered to by the planter. People who don't give invariably try to take up the lion's share of a planter's time. We don't want you to make that mistake.

We want you free to spend time with people who are ready, willing, and able to serve the project in its initial phase. Someone else on the team needs to spend pastoral time with people on the fringe.

> It's been our experience as pastors that people actually stop giving anywhere from six to nine months before they actually leave the church. So knowing what people are giving actually helps in giving the kind of pastoral care needed before the time of dropout.

It's important to note we are making a distinction between members of the launch team and those investigating the community you are gathering. People on your launch team need to be listened to and ministered to by the planter. You need to know their agendas. But you don't need to listen to or know the agendas or ideas of people who have invested marginally of their life in the plant. We don't want you to spend time listening to people who have not yet invested in the project. They have no right to be heard until they show their commitment. If you have a problem with this section, the odds are stacked against you to be an effective church planter.

You Can't Build the Church or Do a Pledge Drive on Tips

I (Jim) still remember my last church plant. About a year into it, a couple showed up. They were a very traditional church family who would never have returned to our church except for what happened that morning. The man brought his sister who was visiting them for the weekend. Although she was raised in the same church as this man, similar to many others she had ceased attending church. To his great sadness, she had just given birth out of wedlock and was in town to discuss adoption proceedings.

At the end of the service she turned to her brother and said, "This was really good. Thanks for bringing me." It undid his entire ecclesiastical world. He's never been the same since.

Upon returning home, she opened up the wound in her heart and began to share with her brother. So he called me up and said, "My wife and I would like to talk to you about the church." So I went to their house.

"I just don't understand this," he said. "This is not like anything I've ever experienced. The service changed my sister's life." And so I spent a couple of hours sharing with this couple.

Finally, he said, "Pastor, what do you need?"

I looked at him and said, "I appreciate your confidence. I need a lot of things; but quite honestly the thing I need the most is, if you haven't committed your tithe elsewhere, to direct it to our new church."

To my amazement, he said, "Okay. What else do you need?"

Planters, not everyone who comes to your church are anti-church or anti-God. They really are often angels sent to you by God. But you have to ask!

Invite Your Networks to Give

Make a list of everyone you know. We mean everyone. Don't leave anyone off. You never know who will be excited about your vision.[4] Send them the sample letter above, and ask them to invest in what you're doing. Be unashamed in this practice, and do it over and over and over and over.

Planter, Raise One Half of Your Salary

Experience has shown that the planters who raise half of their salary prior to planting have the best track record, not because they start with more money, but because they forced themselves to ask and, in so doing, to trust God in bigger ways. We've found many people will give to the planter and not necessarily the plant. Our experience has been that if planters can't raise money, chances are they can't recruit people, because the same skill set is involved in both. The same skill a person needs to recruit people or to win people to his or her cause is basically the same skill needed to raise money for the vision. You're just asking for a different thing. The key is the planter must be willing to ask.[5]

■ ■ ■ SUPERVISORY COMMENTS: Supervisors, take a lesson from the banking world. They make construction loans based on what the contractor has accomplished. Following such a method, the start-up loan or grant for a church plant would be approved, and the entire amount "escrowed." The planter would then be given a large first installment (usually about half) to use however he or she saw fit in the start up phase. However, to qualify for the next round of funding, certain agreed upon "benchmarks" would have to be completed. This is what planter, launch team, coach, and supervisor

---

[4]For more on how to make this list, see Bill Easum and Bil Cornelius, *Go Big: How to Have Explosive Growth in Your Church* (Nashville: Abingdon Press, 2006).
[5]For more on how to make the big ask, see ibid.

would evaluate monthly so that there are no surprises. If the plant has not achieved the primary benchmarks, allocating more money will not solve the problem. So, rather than remove the money from the account, it remains until the benchmark is completed.

Don't pressure the planter to begin before a critical mass is obtained. And don't reduce the amount of money based on the growth of the church. View a church plant as you would view an overseas mission project to non-Christian people. You don't expect that mission project to pay for itself right off the bat. Instead, the missionary is going to be supported from outside. So view the church plant here in the States the same way. If we understand a church plant is about reaching the unchurched, we shouldn't expect the unchurched to support the plant from the beginning.

Also, it doesn't make sense to reduce the funding as the attendance goes up. Remember, as the church grows, it needs more money, and the giving always lags behind the giving in the beginning. Reducing the giving looks like a penalty; the planter is working harder and getting penalized for it. So it's important that the supervisor negotiate the amount of money it will take to grow the church to viability instead of telling the planter there is a fixed amount of money.

Still, just because planters raise virtue capital, that does not give them the right to spend it any way they want. I've (Jim) literally seen millions of dollars misused by planters because no one questioned their spending habits and decisions. You need to constantly inquire how and why they plan to spend the money and give them guidance. If you don't have a clue how to advise them, call in a coach.

● ● ● COACHING COMMENTS: Planters, from day one teach stewardship of money to your launch team and subsequent leaders, and expect people to grow in their financial commitment to God's mission through your church. Do not be afraid of talking about people becoming the master of their money; otherwise, it will be their master. Also make your master list of networks to ask for "virtue capital" and relate to them over and over.

Financial foresight and calculations don't require a great deal of time. However, they do require a good deal of sober thought. The planter is best served at this stage by heeding the advice of people knowledgeable in this area. That is why we recommend having someone on your launch team who understands cash flow and can calculate the financial needs.

For the new and young church, we have these seven instructions:

- Learn the costs and financial standards of your community.
- Along with advisors, calculate the three-year costs.
- Don't equate numerical growth with financial viability.
- Recognize that growth consumes capital.
- Teach giving early and often—it is biblical—and do not confine your teaching to the pulpit.
- Keep the intercessory prayer partners praying for divine appointments and financial miracles.
- Train the launch team to take up the responsibility to raise dollars so this does not fall to the planter alone.

8

Failure of the Church to Act
Its Age and Its Size

On the surface, it appeared to be a great church plant. Attendance was excellent; the pastor was energetic, outgoing, and running a tight, productive, and team-centered ministry. The leadership team he'd assembled was extraordinary, filled with thoughtful, capable, and ambitious innovators. Every one of them was leading programs perfectly suited to their personalities and they appeared to be capable of replicating what was happening.

The team was so good I (Jim) decided to sit with them and talk about what they were doing and how they felt about it.

A few minutes into the interviews, it was painfully clear: every one of the team, from the paid staff to the chair of the board, was pathologically busy. Everyone was exhausted from running the Sunday morning service of worship, Sunday school programs, a Sunday evening "college and careers" supper, Wednesday night Bible study, and a Scout-like program for boys and girls.

Now, guess what? This church was only a year old, but it was acting as if it had been around a long time!

Act Your Age!

When our two daughters were eight and ten years old, they got into my wife's closet and had a "dress up" day. They put on her gowns and her high-heeled shoes and paraded around the living room. They were the cutest things. It was an amazing time for my wife and me, a time when we saw our girls lost in play in a way that would rarely be repeated. Your kids have probably done the same.

Now, what if we had taken them to the mall and allowed them to walk around the mall in their mother's clothes? People would have said, "What's with those parents? Don't they realize their daughters are only children?" They were little girls, all made up in mommy's dresses, shoes, make-up, everything—everything in its place, perfect, as it should be. Except for that one small thing—they were eight and ten.

An adolescent growing up too fast is unattractive, unappealing, and unbecoming, the kind of tragedy that at best makes the kid the brunt of some unsavory jokes, and at worst the object of abuse.

Churches—especially newly started churches—are no different.

Several years ago, I (Jim) was called in to help a three-year-old church plant that had only twenty-seven people. They wanted to me to coach them in how to grow. I knew the pastor had deep-seated problems when in the course of the conversation he referred to one of his members as the "Assistant Sunday School Superintendent." Did you get that? I'm sitting there thinking, "Twenty-seven adults, and he's got an Assistant Sunday School Superintendent?" He had organized his preemie church to look like a full-grown organization. Think of the time and energy invested in the process that could have been invested in reaching more people.

Most new churches struggle just to get their act together by Opening Sunday. But every now and then, some overachiever comes along and is running not only two services, but also

Sunday school classes for K through 12, with nursery and a full slate of programs for the church week. They've already started advertising seminars on church growth—all in just nine months after launch. What kind of church-planting steroids are these people on?

These highly charged church planters are so anxious to succeed they will push their team into programs and plans they aren't ready to undertake. Because the team deeply believes in their pastor's vision, they push ahead and clean up behind the planter. Great plans—but they were plans that didn't fit—*yet.* The church needs time to grow up into them.

While such actions might look good on the surface, they are bad for the plant. Once in a while the super-fast, super church with its super team is for real. But most of these super churches and super teams are a bunch of eight- and ten-year-old girls running through the mall all dressed up like their moms.

Nobody in a church plant is playing dress-up. Church planting is real-life drama that requires leaders and the church to act its age and size. Sure, they were doing the right thing, but at the wrong time. Their impatience was leading down a path that could only wind up in exhaustion and loss of a great team of leaders. People can work a hundred hours a week for just so long.

Often when I'm (Jim) called in by a denomination or group to do a biopsy of a church in trouble, or an autopsy of a failed plant, this mistake shows. You can see the symptoms everywhere, especially in the exhausted and weary "launch team" members trying to play catch up with the new programs they "had" to launch.

You'll hear the evidence in the comments of the pastor or the parishioners or team members, all of them wanting "to be an 'adult'...*now*" and offering up arguments that are, in many ways, tough to respond to.

"Don't you need to take risks?"

"Don't we need to 'step out in faith'?"

Yes, you do. Any church plant will have to go a bit ahead of where they are at some point in their journey toward adulthood. But when you do, you'd better make sure your risks and faith are part of a reasonable, developmental philosophy.

You Have to Let Some People Walk Away

We understand the temptation and the pressure to have all the ministries in place before launching. We see it all the time. You're three-weeks-old, meeting at a middle school, and a family comes in the door with three kids. The family has just relocated to the community from a full-service church. The first thing they ask is, "What do you have for my two-year-old and my middle school teenager? And, oh, by the way, my elderly grandmother's with us. What do you have for her?"

Effective church plants don't begin ministries to please guests. It's better to just let them walk away than to overextend and burn out. It's also better than making promises you can't keep. Making promises you can't keep undermines your credibility over the long term.

I (Jim) remember a family visiting one of the plants I was doing. They visited twice and asked for a meeting. We spent an evening relating stories and answering questions. Their three teens were in high school, and the inevitable question they asked me was, "What's your high school ministry like?" To which I replied, "We don't have a high school ministry…"—and then came my mistake—"but we hope to have one up and running within the next three months." Forgive me, but I couldn't help myself. I so much wanted to have this family remain in our young church. They were a great family, they had lots to offer, and I liked them! So, six months later, when the student ministry still hadn't materialized, imagine the hurt I felt when the couple said to me, "You promised." I never saw them again.

Don't try to launch with a handful of people and try to act like a full-service church. One way or another, it will ruin you.

Staying Healthy

More and more emphasis is being given these days to the overall health of the church planter and family. The health of the church plant is in direct proportion to the health of the lead pastor and his or her family, and the staff. If any aspect of their lives is out of balance, sooner or later it will show up in the church. If the planter is constantly pushing the leaders to expand beyond the age or size of the church, more than just physical exhaustion occurs. It is essential the church planter find some balance in his or her life. This means having time for one's personal needs and those of the family.

The Fix: Avoiding the Mistake

Decide on the essential ministries for your particular mission field, and delay all others until they are necessary. Over time, you'll layer in new ministries and expand what you offer as you grow.

Ways to Act Your Age and Size

- Understand your new community and its needs, and treat it as a mission field. Let it define the majority of your goals.
- List the essential ministries you're going to need the day you open for public services.
- Ask, "What are the few specific things we do really well?"
- Teach your people to say, "We're not there yet."
- Understand that some people who visit actually do "need" a full-service church and may leave. Let them.
- Set a goal of creating something sustainable, something that can survive any program launch or new initiative.

"If we had a dollar for every person who said to us, 'Once you get that ministry in place, we'll come to your church,' we'd be rich."

If you're doing even a reasonable job once you've actually launched successfully, new people will drop by all the time. Many of these people will be amazing, gracious, extraordinary believers, anxious to get involved in your new congregation and will bring all sorts of great gifts to your new community. But along with their gifts and skills and imaginations, they also bring expectations—every single one of them. After years of belonging to other churches or watching churches and listening to other believers, these new members of your team will have all sorts of preconceived notions of what a church should do around and for them.

So, just suck it up and say, "*We're not there yet.*"

Everyone has preconceived expectations about churches. Even your super laypersons might ask for more. And they won't necessarily be asking for bad or superficial or superfluous things. All they're expecting is for you to have all the other things the other churches they've been a part of have had. They'll want something good that's probably already on your wish list for the future, and if you're not careful, despite what you know to be wise, you'll cater to the "consumer" demands of your "clients" and start that program. And so it begins. The first stone of a landslide, the mistake that teeters on the verge of a fatal mistake—you let something other than wise planning and the Spirit lead you.

New church members simply don't understand the difference between a church plant and an established church. They have even less of a clue about the vast amount of time, energy, and staff power that starting up any new program requires.

I (Jim) remember a new church I had helped in the Midwest. It was a good plant, doing well and moving along at a very brisk pace. After only a few months, they were carefully adding programs with both grace and wisdom, and growing consistently under the leadership of Bill and Susan and their team of core leaders.

About six months after their launch, John and Patricia, one of the church's core families, brought some friends to the

Sunday services. This family was well-known, well-heeled, and prominent in the community. When they met the pastor at the door at the end of the service, the man took the pastor aside and made two things immediately clear. First, they had been genuinely moved by the service. Second, they made it clear that, if they were going to join, it would be only when there was a youth group to meet the needs of their three teenage kids.

These remarks presented Bill and the team with a kind of quandary. If this family came to their church, more would come, no doubt. But if they created a full-blown youth ministry in a church that had a total of nine children, most of whom were under third grade, what would this say to the existing congregation?

Bill labored under that one for a while. Eventually he and his team chose not to start a youth program at that time, but instead to keep with their original focus and do what they did well. That is what all new churches *must* do to succeed. Every single plant must choose the "essential ministries" that will give definition and guidance to their first few months of development, and stick with them. If you do this it will help your church be developmentally sound.

■ ■ ■ SUPERVISORY SIDEBAR: Don't push the church to charter or develop by-laws or be a full service church from the beginning. Give the church room to grow into the ministries. Guide the planter's pace. Don't argue with the specific goal a planter creates, but do argue with the proposed pace for achieving that goal, whatever number and time frame. Push for a more gracious schedule, negotiate expectations, and keep everyone thinking soberly.

● ● ● COACHING SIDEBAR: We've noticed two telltale signs that indicate a church planter is bowing to the pressure to grow up too fast, too soon:

- a significant alteration of the game plan

- a drastic change of style, usually in the area of music and liturgy

As the planter gathers the new community, her or she needs to be a good steward of people resources. People have much more to do with their time than dedicate themselves wholly to the task of starting a church. They must be allowed to have a life. Many times, planters lose very healthy people because planters set a pace that is not sustainable physically, spiritually, or relationally.

Encourage the planter to always think in terms of intentional, careful, prudent steps. Don't just say, "we want twenty cell groups," and talk about the ultimate dream. You need to be exacting in your language, lest you express your vision as a *promise,* instead of as a *vision.* Shape your goals in the context of a process that includes a reasonable plan. Always think developmentally. Talk about the process to get there. If you announce your goals too early, you run the risk of not creating the broad, exciting dream that will empower and excite your team and congregation. Instead, you will create expectations too soon and discourage your team, creating a credibility gap where one doesn't need to be.

9

Formalizing Leadership Too Soon

Jerome knew it was wrong. His gut instinct told him not to do it, but everyone was clamoring for him to do it. After all, how can the plant be a real church without doing it?

Bill couldn't wait. It just didn't feel like a church yet. He'd worked so hard gathering a crowd and turning it into community, but still it didn't seem like church to him. It was time to do it.

Frustrated in her lack of progress with leaders, Jan reasoned, "If I make them part of an official board, they will take their responsibility more seriously."

When Gilbert found himself stymied by certain "blockers" in his new start, he figured, "If I place these people on the board, they will see what we're facing and be more supportive of me."

Superintendent Rob wanted to show how much progress he'd made in his first year on the job, including a number of new starts, so he pressured one of his churches to "charter" too soon, asking them to be present at the annual denominational gathering. He forced the project's point person, Matt, into placing unregenerate people in positions of spiritual leadership.

Much to the dismay of everyone, the project got bogged down in details with neophytes trying to run a church, and lost momentum. The plant no longer exists.

Formalizing the leadership and organization of the church too soon is dangerous. Whether it's bowing to pressure by zealous supervisors, current "unofficial" leaders, personal insecurities, or personal experience with a previous "church," the net effect is the same—a major sea change in the life of the church, and, more importantly, redirecting youthful energies away from mission to management. Either way, formalizing leadership too soon *always* hinders the growth of a plant. The organization of the plant needs time to find its indigenous roots in the mission field. Future leaders need time to prove themselves on the battlefield.

You Don't Need More Leaders at First

It's been our experience that those who start with the project bring lots of energy to the launch, but not necessarily the much-needed strengths to organize and manage it in such a way as to keep it moving. In the early stages of a plant you need people who will do what you ask, show up on time, serve joyously, and don't expect anything from you. We remind planters all the time, "You're the leader. You don't need more leaders right now; you need workers!"

You may be asking, "But what about accountability?" One of the most common myths says that all planters have been infected with the "independence" gene and rebel against any form of authority. Nothing could be further from our experience. Most planters understand they are under authority. They seek out and invite mentors to speak into their lives. They have a coach and ask lots of questions. Those questioning the planter's authority often mean, "When are you going to do what I want you to do?" or, "When are you going to report to me about that strategy, so that I can give my input?" Many planters we've coached have encountered this. We tell them to deter this kind of inquisition with this reply: "I report directly to my supervisor and coach and never do anything without first running it by them." We also tell planters that those who ask, "When are we going to have leaders?" are really asking, "When do I get to be part of having a say in the running of the church?" Avoid placing any such people in an official position of leadership in the church. Usually after the first board members are chosen, this modern-day "Diotrephes" leaves for greener pastures.[1]

Leaders Must Prove Themselves in Your Plant

The New Testament says you should give leadership to people who have proven themselves in your church, not because they've proven themselves in someone else's church.[2] People must earn the reputation of being a leader *within your church plant*. That way the congregation sees the person exercising leadership and affirms them by putting them into a position of authority. Just because that person was considered an effective leader in some other church doesn't mean he or she will measure up to your standards or to the needs of your mission field.

Discovering leadership takes time. You won't know who your key leaders are when you launch. They may or may not be on your launch team. Only over time will the real leaders come to the surface. How long should you wait to formalize leadership? We know there are exceptions, but as a general rule, we recommend the process begin sometime in the third year after your public launch.

We need to say this loud and clear—*be careful whom you put into leadership*. If somebody comes to you and says, "When are we going to have elders or deacons or lay leaders?" or, "When are we going to have a counsel or board or vestry or session?"

---

[1] Referring to 3 John 9–11: "I wrote something to the church; but Diotrephes, who loves to be first among them, does not accept what we say. For this reason, if I come, I will call attention to his deeds which he does, unjustly accusing us with wicked words; and not satisfied with this, he himself does not receive the brethren, either, and he forbids those who desire to do so and puts them out of the church. Beloved, do not imitate what is evil, but what is good. The one who does good is of God; the one who does evil has not seen God" (NASB).

[2] "Therefore, brethren, select from among you seven men of good reputation" (Acts 6:3a, NASB).

write that person's name down. Beside that name write, "This person will never serve in an official capacity in this church." The real issue behind these questions is a grab for power. That person really wants to be on your board, and someone that anxious to be in a position of power is the last person you want in that position.

You Do Not Need Official Board Members to Run Ministries

On the advice of his supervisor, Mike proceeded to appoint an official board, adopt a constitution and by-laws, and ask people to become "charter members"—all within six months of the church launch. His supervisor told Mike to bring on at least ten board members so that each area of responsibility in the church was covered. Mike, being the compliant person he was, acquiesced to the request of his supervisor.

Unfortunately, all the easy, natural, and intuitive decisions Mike made on a regular basis now came under the microscope of his newly approved board. The loud screeching sound was from the momentum and enthusiasm as the new church took a hard right turn on two wheels, careening onto a side road leading to lesser roads that terminated at a cul-de-sac, followed by more wrong turns and more cul-de-sacs.

Decisions now took weeks; creativity declined; and fresh ideas grew stale and came less and less often. One day six months later, Mike found himself ruing the day he'd agreed to have board members. Worn out, he resigned, leaving the church to people focused solely on the organization.

Delay Organizing

Registering as a formal entity is quite different from organizing your new start. Of course you have to organize who's leading what, who's in charge of what, and monitor the progress of key ministries. But here's the operative concept: all of this happens around the ministries of the new church. Everyone is on the front lines, doing something; no one is "back in the office" making the decisions. This setup is quite different from nominating committees and bureaucrats whose premature existence in the project only serves to frustrate the planter.

Just like discovering your leaders, it takes time to discover the best organizational structure for your church. You may have a good idea of what it might look like in the beginning. But as you tweak your vision to fit the mission field, you will find a better way to organize around your DNA.

For churches renting facilities, we recommend hiring a part-time facilities supervisor from among the best leaders. This person takes responsibility for getting the teams together to have everything ready for weekly worship without involving the launch team or the pastor.

How to Select Your First Board

First Timothy 3 gives the necessary general criteria for anyone serving in spiritual leadership of a church. The person

- is not a new convert
- has self-control—over emotions, tongue, drink, and money
- is a proven manager (manages his or her household well)

When it comes to selecting the first board members of a new church, two more non-negotiables are best required:

- loyalty to the planter
- a tither, not a tipper to the work. Jesus reminds us, "where your treasure is, there will your heart will be also" (Mt. 6:21). Anyone worthy of serving on a board should exhibit financial commitment to that church.

We're not recommending "blind" loyalty. We're referring to the kind of loyalty found in Proverbs: "Faithful are the wounds of a friend, But deceitful are the kisses of an enemy" (27:6,

NASB). The biblical writer suggests that some people will tell you what you want to hear, *but they are not your friends*. On the other hand, some people love you so much, they will speak words that may wound you, *because you need to hear them.*

The Process for Selecting the Board

This process should take about three to five months.

- Write a letter informing the congregation that in this ministry year you will be forming the first official board.
- Ask them to submit names for consideration—do not use the word "nominate" (they are not the ad hoc nominating committee).
- Give a deadline of no more than three weeks in which to submit names.
- List what is expected of every board member.
- List the criteria by which they should identify people whom they may want to be considered. (This is somewhat subject to one's tribal guidelines and theological persuasion.). For a starting point, see above criteria from 1 Timothy 3.
- Once the names are given, the planter functions as a nominating committee of one.
- When needing input, seek counsel from outside the group.
- Keep the first board small in number. We suggest no more than three to five people.
- Stagger the terms from the beginning, with a minimum of two years at the outset.
- Don't add any more new people for at least two more years. In rare cases, making changes or additions too early interrupts the flow of the group learning to work together.
- We suggest selecting and commissioning the leaders prior to the church charter or constitution. We know this goes against many by-laws and institutional thinking, but our experience in watching these things unfold tells us it works better this way.

- After finalizing a list of possible board members, contact them about their willingness to enter into an examination process to see if they meet the criteria. Include the list of expectations that went out in the letter to the entire congregation.
- Set up a personal meeting with each of them, and, if they are married, with their spouses, to answer any questions they may have about what is expected of them.
- Conduct follow-up personal meetings with them to discuss any issues that might have come up in the process.
- Ask for permission to move forward with their names to the congregation.
- Within eight to twelve weeks of sending out the initial letter, send a second letter listing the persons you want considered as board members.
- Instruct the congregation to contact you, or your supervisor, if they have reservations about anyone on the list. (Failure to do this will result in either a blind spot that is ignored, or set a precedent of stifling feedback.) Give a deadline for feedback.
- Once the list is finalized, send out a third mailing, putting forth the names of the individuals placed in consideration for becoming official board members.
- If you decide to have a vote on this, announce the deadline (usually within three weeks) and have it immediately following the worship service. (An easy way to do this would be to have the worship dismissal, announcing a reconvening in five minutes.) In this day of the Internet, many churches can now also ask members to e-mail their votes.
- The slate of people should be not as individuals, but as a group.
- On the ballot, ask the congregation to either "accept" or "reject" the group.
- Set a time to "commission" the new board members. (Do this during the regularly scheduled worship service to model for your congregation how churches conduct matters). Invite some area pastors or leaders to participate in this time.

The Fix: Avoiding the Mistake

Everyone needs some form of accountability. What you don't need is a group from which you have to get permission to act. So, in the early years put together a small advisory team. Call it a task force, or advisory team, or an ad hoc group. Don't call it a board and turn them into a group from which you have to get permission to act. You don't need any form of a board in the early years.

So remember, anytime you have a group meet at a regularly scheduled day and time, you begin to turn it into an official-looking and official-acting group. This invites misinterpretation. I (Jim) coach a planter now (2007) who had an ad hoc group that met regularly for two and a half years. Last fall they selected their first official board. One of the individuals from the ad hoc group was not selected to participate on the official board. Upon receiving notice that he would not be asked, he left the church.

The planter was devastated, wondering what he had done to cause such a reaction. The problem was twofold: one, the group had been meeting so regularly that the person considered himself to be already a member of the board; and two, the situation revealed something about the character and agenda of the person seeking office. Although no one can be sure why the person left the church, the planter must offer thanks to God for revealing the person's real character before the person was asked to serve in an official capacity.

Keep your board size as small as possible. The smaller the board, the larger the church has the chance of becoming. It's not unusual today for a church of ten to twenty thousand to have only a handful of people on their boards.

Don't charter or develop by-laws and a constitution until it is absolutely necessary. Many people enjoy getting in on the ground floor, but that doesn't mean they know how to oversee and manage. Remember, leaders need to have spiritual maturity before they are put into any official capacity.

■ ■ ■ SUPERVISORY COMMENTS: Don't push your planters to charter and develop a board until at least the third year of the public launch. Encourage them to keep the board as small as possible and only put proven leaders in positions of authority.

● ● ● COACHING COMMENTS: Walk the planter through the sequential steps necessary in the selection process. Force the planter to make choices and justify them by applying this principle: "The best indicator of future performance is current and past performance." There's no room for the planter to speak in terms of someone's "potential." Instead, demand evidence from the planter that these folks are already leaders at the planter's church.

10

Using the "Superstar" Model as the Paradigm for All Church Plants

James had the opportunity to attend one of the megachurches near him. While worshiping, he found himself saying, "I want to plant that kind of church." On returning home, he went online and registered for the megachurch's upcoming workshop. Just driving into the parking lot, he began to drool. Well-placed signage and easily identified parking lot attendants guided him effortlessly to a spot. Parking his car, he joined other conference attendees as they made their way toward the welcoming facilities. Warmly welcomed by a greeter at the door, he made his way to the registration table, where smart-dressed volunteers processed his registration and helped him gather up his materials.

James could hardly contain himself as he walked into the large meeting space, tastefully decorated and teeming with activity. People stood around talking excitedly as the latest Christian artist blared over the sound system. He almost leapt out of his seat as the worship band cranked up and the worship leader led everyone in the opening song. He found his parched spirit beginning to fill with energy and life, something he'd missed in his life of ministering in churches that would turn up their noses at such a setting.

As the final benediction was given, James sat in his seat and wept. How he missed this kind of experience. All he could think was, "I was meant for this!" Then something happened to James that week. In his zeal at finding his spirit reawakened, his exclamation of, "I was meant for this," turned into a declaration of, "I want this."

Back home, James's thoughts increasingly turned to his experience. His declaration, "I want this," turned to, "I have to have this," and finally to, "I can't be true to myself if I don't do this." He sat down one evening and, in Jerry Maguire like fashion, formulated his mission statement by revisiting the many notes he'd taken at the conference and by visiting the sponsoring church's Web site to "cut and paste" their values. In a very short time he'd fashioned his "vision."

With that, he began to plan and pray and find like-minded people. He'd articulate the vision to them, sharing his journey of frustration and enlightenment, and close with the question, "Don't you want this also?" Each time someone joined his small band, his expectations and goals increased.

James and his launch team began to study and plan what he had learned at the conference. They visited a few other churches and workshops and soon had a full "hybrid," tweaking the vision and plan as they went. Whenever a question arose in the group that couldn't be answered, they consulted the "experts." Word spread that a church "just like X" was opening. More people signed on.

With much fanfare they launched, experiencing a certain measure of success; and even if they hadn't, they had a good plan, and, even better, the plan had worked for others.

The famous last words of a failed plant: "But 'Willow-Back-Burg-Rez-Hill-Village-House-Ship-Point' did it this way!"

Some leaders get stuck on one way to plant churches. We

think that's a major mistake—the context of ministry should determine the model. This chapter is about the indiscriminate use of methods and styles with little or no thought to the mission field and context. Even worse, this use betrays the insidious practice of "cutting and pasting" someone else's story into the story that *God* wants to write through the planter and launch team.

One of the realities all church plants face is the post-launch phase when people's excitement turns to reasonable reflection and they begin to evaluate progress. If the launch team finds the progress tepid or faltering, morale becomes the church planter's primary focus; and the mission of reaching those outside the fold quickly turns into fighting inertia. Almost one half of the autopsies I've (Jim) conducted, the church had made the mistake of thinking they could "cut and paste" their way to success in church planting.

It's our contention that God gets blamed far too often for a vision that God did not give. Many of these so-called "visions" came from the desires and appetites of good men and women starved to make an impact in the kingdom of God. We've seen too many who have tried to plant a church on someone else's vision. Rather than go into their own closet and get on their knees with a clean heart before God and with Holy Scripture opened, and not leave until receiving a word from on High, today's church planters are too quick to settle for someone else's vision.

You CANNOT plant a church on a "borrowed" vision.

James made the mistake of Xeroxing someone else's vision rather than developing his own vision that was indigenous to his mission field. During countless debriefings, I've (Jim) had planters say to me, "But so and so [quoting some great church leader] did it this way, and it worked for them!" I have to contain myself, while saying to them, "Well, I hate to be the bearer of bad news, but you're *not* 'so and so'; and your situation isn't their situation. You simply cannot plant a church on a 'borrowed' vision.' It must be yours and be how God has gifted you."

Having conducted more than 1,900 assessments of clergy wanting to plant a church, I've (Jim) seen many who did not have the essential competencies to do what their vision entailed. For example, I once interviewed a couple who could barely contain their zeal for reaching "unchurched seekers" in their proposed new start project. As the young man detailed his "heart" and "passion" to reach these people, I was moved. But I was not convinced.

Since their vision involved the frequent contacting and networking of lots of unchurched, non-Christian, antagonistic to the gospel people, I asked them, "When was the last time you intentionally invited into your home someone like you've just described?" They looked perplexed, as if to say, "What do you mean?" I explained that since they had requested significant funding for their plan, it would be a good idea to see what patterns of reaching "unchurched seekers" they had already put into place in their current ministry situation.

They had never entertained one person like this, in their home or anywhere else. I then asked them to tell me the last time they had a conversation with such a person in which they discussed their spiritual journey and how the gospel of Christ impacted such a journey. Again I was met with puzzled looks.

I then asked them a final question, "Based on your vision to reach people who have little or no church background and who rarely would frequent a traditional-looking church building, 'When you're in a restaurant, do you two wait in the "lounge" section before being called to your table?'" The next day I found out this question offended them deeply. They called their regional director and asked him, "Was the man you sent to interview us really a Christian, because he asked us if we ever went to a bar!"

This young couple didn't have a vision from God. This

couple had borne no "fruit" whatsoever in reaching those whom they had proposed to reach, and then claimed the vision was from God. In the assessment business we have a saying, "What's going to change besides the area code and zip code?" For this couple, applying for a significant monetary grant, the denomination had been three questions away from funding a fantasy.

Any funding group should abide by this rule: "We fund fruit, not fantasies."

The best church planters and pastors never let someone else's vision substitute for the hard work of packing up and going into the closet to pray. I (Jim) still recall the time when, along with the other student ministry leaders, I sat transfixed as Bill Hybels shared the vision God had given him while writing a research paper holed up in his dad's company condo by Lake Michigan. He was all of twenty-two, but his heart had sought after God, and God had answered. As many have said since, "Who'd a-thunk it?"

The Vineyard Church in Cincinnati is a great church with a great heart. The first pastor founded the church on doing random acts of kindness.[1] People cleaned toilets, gave away bottled water, cleaned up cigarette butts off the freeway exits, and participated in a host of other projects, all for free. That ministry alone catapulted the church into one of the largest churches in the United States. Over the years since, we have seen pastors of church plants become enamored with this ministry and implement it in their churches, only to fall on their faces. It didn't work for them because it didn't come from their hearts.

The Fix: Avoiding the Mistake

You must allow the mission field, rather than some effective church, guide your decisions. You simply can't "cut and paste"

---

[1]See www.kindness.com.

your way to effectiveness. Never become so enamored by what someone else is doing in ministry that your goal is to replicate what they are doing. Instead, your goal is to plant an indigenous church that comes out of personal reflection, fine tuned by mentors and trainers, and adapted to the people in the mission field. Anything less won't have a chance.

■ ■ ■ SUPERVISORY COMMENTS: Far too many assessments and hires begin with a preconceived "model" and then attempt to force it on the mission field. What gets measured is "affinity" for the model, not "ability to bear fruit" in the mission field.

The worst thing you can do is to fund such a fantasy vision. You should create an indigenous assessment system that forces people to take a sober look at what they are proposing and forces the candidates to demonstrate a "track record" for the kind of ministry being articulated on paper. By starting with the demographics of the mission field and the type of new start being attempted, a healthy process assesses affinities and experiences in similar settings, along with bearing fruit. The unexamined vision is not worth funding.

Also, avoid telling the planter, "This is the kind of church I want you to plant," and then showing the planter a picture of a church from some other part of the country.

● ● ● COACHING COMMENTS: Before signing on to coach a project, make sure the "model" actually fits the mission field and the planter has the competencies to do what's expected of him or her. Countless times, doing my (Jim) interview with supervisor and planter, I've discovered a disconnect between the model being presented and the expectations put forth. At that time, I call a timeout and begin to ask questions that force them to face some measure of reality. Ask the planter, "Is the project indigenous to its context? Do God's fingerprints appear in the process?" Granted, these questions are somewhat subjective; nevertheless, they are valid because they can root out any "cutting and pasting" type of fantasy. It's been our experience that if God's fingerprints aren't evident in the impulse to plant, nothing is going to change. I cannot tell you the number of times when my questions have been received as "attacks" on God's vision. Nevertheless, I press forward, asking questions that force behavioral answers.

Coaches, remember that you can walk away graciously from the project. Just because they want your services and expertise doesn't obligate you to say yes.

Moving on into the Mission Field

Planter, you have to plant in the way you are experiencing God leading you, not how someone else has done it or told you how to do it. Church planting is hard enough without trying to replicate what someone else did.

Make sure what you plan to do is what God wants done. That way it will meet the need of the mission field. If God has anointed you to plant a church, God will give you the vision, the wiring, and the abilities to do it God's way.

Congratulations!

Congratulations on finishing the book. Now you know the top ten mistakes planters make and can make the necessary adjustments to either correct them or avoid them. It's been our pleasure to walk you through what we've learned over the years. It's our prayer that you will find God's fingerprints in these pages.

What you are about is the most glorious work in the universe. We applaud you for your desire to plant. But we now ask you to go off into a quiet place and search your soul for God's leadership. And if you still feel called to plant, then do so with all your being.

If either of us can be of help in the process, you can contact us at the following:

Jim Griffith— jim@griffithcoaching.com
Bill Easum – easum@easumbandy.com

Now, what's keeping you from the journey?

APPENDIX

Taking a Public Offering

One of the most misunderstood topics in public services, both for existing churches and emerging congregations, is the idea that taking a public offering is offensive to the unchurched. I have found this personally and formally to be very far from the truth.

Jesus spoke more about the use of our earthly resources ("treasures") than he did about eternity, so the means by which you highlight this will determine the fullness with which the unchurched grasp that being a disciple of Jesus includes coming to grips with God's sovereignty over the management and disbursement of one's resources. In effect, many churches desiring to communicate the message of Jesus inadvertently subordinate one of his major teachings.

The primary issue is the inept and indiscriminate way in which churches take the offering. In the five churches I (Jim) planted and the churches I've coached, I've yet to see the unchurched be offended, or, even worse, confused, by the offering, if two rules were followed:

1. An appropriate and tasteful explanation is provided. Take the time to train your spokespersons in this. See below the script that we developed and have used over the years, both personally and in the churches I've coached:

We come to that time in the service where we take the offering. For those of you who are visiting, please feel no obligation to participate. This service is our gift to you. But for those of you who consider X Church to be your church home, we want to thank you for your faithfulness to participate financially in the ongoing support of this ministry.

2. You only need one rule for the Offering Etiquette:

DO NOT DEVIATE FROM THE SCRIPT
(Some spokespersons feel they have to be apologetic)

DO NOT DEVIATE FROM THE SCRIPT
(Some spokespersons feel that more explanation is needed)

DO NOT DEVIATE FROM THE SCRIPT
(Some spokespersons feel the need to "teach" on stewardship during this time)

DO NOT DEVIATE FROM THE SCRIPT
(Some spokespersons feel this is the time to rail against financial excess)

DO NOT DEVIATE FROM THE SCRIPT
(Some spokespersons feel this is the slot to make urgent appeals)

Also, the collectors of the offering start the collection plate at the front and then immediately proceed to the rear of the room.

Three Excellent Resources on Financial Stewardship

- Financial Peace University, www.daeramsey.com
- Willow Creek Community Church, www.goodsenseministry.com
- Crown Ministries, www.crown.org

Response Card

I want to increase the percentage I give to God in order to help Spring of Life "Stand On Our Own" in 2006.

Here's my pledge for 2006:

5% _____

8% _____

10%_____

Other _____

What % Do I Give?

	5%	8%	10%	12%
$30,000	1,500	2,400	3,000	3,600
$40,000	2,000	3,200	4,000	4,800
$50,000	2,500	4,000	5,000	6,000
$60,000	3,000	4,800	6,000	7,200
$70,000	3,500	5,600	7,000	8,400
$80,000	4,000	6,400	8,000	9,600

"Bring the whole tithe into the storehouse, that there may be food in my house. Test me in this," says the LORD Almighty, "and see if I will not throw open the floodgates of heaven and pour out so much blessing that you will not have room enough for it." (Malachi 3:10)

Response Card

My contribution to God's work at Spring of Life year to date is $_____.

Our fair share amount to meet operational ministry goals in 2006 is $200 per person/month.

I want to help Spring of Life "Stand On Our Own" in 2006.

Here's my pledge for 2006:

$100/month _____

$150/month _____

$200/month _____

$_____/month _____

Each of you must give as you have made up your mind, not reluctantly or under compulsion, for God loves a cheerful giver. (2 Corinthians 9:7)

Response Card

My contribution to God's work at _____ year to date is $_____.

I want to help Spring of Life "Stand On Our Own" in 2006.

Here's my pledge for 2006 $_____

Here's my one-time gift for 2006 $_____.

Each of you must give as you have made up your mind, not reluctantly or under compulsion, for God loves a cheerful giver. (2 Corinthians 9:7)